DRIVING RESULTS THROUGH OTHERS:

A Pocket Guide for Learning on the Job

Christine Haskell, PHD

Run for Cover Publishing, LLC

SEATTLE

Driving Results Through Others: A Pocket Guide for Learning on the Job

© 2021 Christine Haskell

No part of this work may be reproduced or transmitted in any form without the prior written authorization of the author unless the copying is expressly permitted by federal copyright law.

All rights reserved.

ISBN: 978-1-7329081-2-3

EBOOK ISBN: 978-1-7329081-3-0

Cover design, interior design and illustrations: Rob Nance

For information about special discounts for bulk purchases, please visit: www.runforcoverpress.com

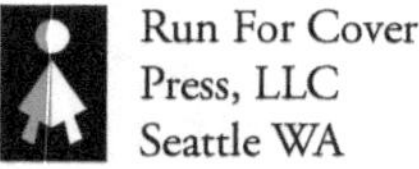

Run For Cover
Press, LLC
Seattle WA

Note From the Author

This little pocket guide was developed by observing and synthesizing common questions from my clients as they encountered obstacles familiar to all of us—the manager who keeps moving the goal posts, an un-collaborative colleague, negativity, criticism, or people that are just hard to work with.

Senior technology leaders need to constantly be driving change and confronting challenges to manage growth—all while developing themselves and their teams. Supervisors and mechanics on naval shipyards need to innovate and customize tools in real time to deliver naval war ships on time and under budget. Regardless of where we work, everyone must navigate for buy-in or approval in dense, interconnected systems.

As a former manager myself, I have lived through many of these scenarios and can empathize with how hard it is to be on the hook for achieving results, while also learning how to lead people. And, I've made mistakes. Seeing challenge without also seeing opportunity didn't serve me because it took away from my performance rather than enhanced it.

Everyone—from the CEO to the intern—learns on the job. It's one thing thinking through an effective process, but once people get involved and the pressures of deadlines and budgets are included, those processes are actually *felt* by everyone. Effectiveness is an individual skill, first. Across every sector and every level of leadership, there is a common need to effectively work with others.

To perform well while under pressure, we need to train our minds to work more effectively. Making the right decisions—whether that is hashing out how artificial intelligence will evolve in a social media company or ensuring naval ships are ready on time—takes *practice*. I hope these very universal questions and practical answers provide the simple reminders we all need for how to get started with your own mind-training practice.

Christine Haskell, Ph.D.

Contents

Introduction

The terms *mind frame* and *mindset* are being talked about a lot lately—and with good reason. *The quality of everything we do depends on the quality of the thinking we do first.* A chilling thought because the implications are enormous. A critical takeaway is that there is nothing—*nothing*—more important in developing individual and organizational effectiveness than ensuring that people *think for themselves* with rigor, imagination, and courage. Every day, in every meeting, and in every interaction.

When we are under pressure, our minds are not fully functional. We are, quite literally, not in the "right frame of mind." When we feel pressure, threat, or discomfort with change, we are likely to react rather than respond. Our thinking and decision making are out of focus. We are quick to judge. Our field of vision narrows. We selectively pull data from our environments through this hyper-focused, lopsided, and narrow lens. With our sense of reality distorted, we cannot accurately diagnose what is going on. Our mental processes are consumed by judgment and reactivity rather than objective observation and appropriate action. Trapped by our own minds, we cannot achieve the results we want.

Effectiveness, accountability, performance—these are mindsets, not skillsets. Mindsets are about the way we experience life. For example, we can look at success and failure (or rather, success and "Not Yet"). We need to start looking at change as just something that needs to happen and will *continue* happening. We must learn to accept difficulty as just part of the process and not see it as a discreet event or specific phase to avoid.

We've all suffered difficulty and crossed paths with people we perceive to be prickly, difficult, challenging, irritating, frustrating, infuriating and uncooperative. There will always be those whose temperaments, values, habits, and character flaws that chafe with our own. But when it really comes down to it, most people will have different goals than us and *that* is often what gets in the way when we are trying to work with and through others. We want to make a process more efficient; those we are trying to influence see learning a new approach as a tax on their time. Whether we want them to or not, challenges weave themselves into our lives. It's up to us to find ways to manage the headaches, heartbreaks, chaos, and stress we perceive them as creating for us (and potentially others). The ideas found in this little pocket guide can help us withstand those challenging relationships without going crazy or over compromising.

You Might Experience Others As Challenging, When:

Experiencing challenge can mean many things to many people—it's what is challenging to *you*. Maybe it's...

- a manager who keeps moving the goal posts

- an un-collaborative colleague

- a negative friend

- a critical family member

- someone who is just hard to get along with

How Do We Get Along With Them?

Practicing empathy, curiosity, and patience slows the conversation down. Slowing a conversation is likely to increase possibilities and alternatives. Slowing down decreases reactivity. When we are less reactive, we don't experience other *as* difficult or *as* challenging as we might when we are irked by something they said. We are capable of thinking more creatively about what might be happening. Perhaps the…

- manager received new directives and needs to adjust, requiring everyone else to adjust

- un-collaborative friend has a competing commitment requiring a strategy alignment

- negative friend has low confidence about their abilities or is afraid of making mistakes

- critical family member regrets their past actions or errors in judgment, and is struggling to forgive themselves

- person who is hard to get along with struggles with themselves, too, habitually blaming others for their sense of powerlessness

The real answer is, we just never know. But our judgement of them is rarely the whole story.

Benefits Of Learning To Drive Results With Others:

This guide will help you to:

- Understand what makes people tick and how best to manage your own experience with them;

- Learn ways to confidently maintain your boundaries with others and resist the urge to attack back;

- Develop strategies to calmly navigate emotionally charged situations;

- Deal with all kinds of people, in a variety of situations;

- Find it easier to form and maintain interpersonal relationships and to '*fit in*' to group situations;

- Know when to choose your battles, and when to walk away; and,

- Become exposed to a number of tools and strategies to help you develop your own ongoing practice.

When we react, we need to distinguish what is and is not in our control. When confronted by challenge or change, our immediate response is to react. Our first thoughts during our reactions are never our fault. The thoughts racing through our minds are part of our wiring and ways of coping.

However, our judgments, impulses, will, and choices are all within our control. Just because these things are within our control doesn't mean they aren't influenced by external factors, such as other people's opinions of us, or physical sensations, etc. But ultimately, our reactions to challenge and change are under our control because we can make a conscious choice to ignore our impulses or override the opinions of others.

There are things not in our control: how our body reacts, our property could get damaged or stolen, our reputation is in the hands of others, and anything that is not our own doing (basically all things external to our mind). There's an argument that these things are under our partial control, and that's true, but the main takeaway is: greater self-management skills lead to greater effectiveness and better performance, in ourselves and others.

Think about times when we've perceived people we need to influence as under-performing. How did we manage our reactivity? Did we try to help? Were we resentful? And, are we being honest in how we answer these questions?

Leaders who are responsible for a team's outcome will most often answer that they try to help. We want to think the best of ourselves. And, maybe we do help, a few times. Eventually though, after enough failed attempts, we might start to expect less from our staff. We might start to imagine poor performers would find their own way off the team. We accept less quality or output from others and resent them for it. We can sulk, become defensive, or attack. But there are smarter moves to make when trying to drive results through others.

The concepts in this guide will explain how to cope in a range of situations and focus on what we can change (about ourselves, first). For those trying to maintain a reflective practice, there are questions to discuss with others and journal prompts to consider as our self-awareness deepens.

There are many, many ways to ground ourselves amidst conflict. Some turn to their faith, others meditate, go to the gym, engage in community sports, do art projects, or read. Whatever the activity, it's important to know what tools work, *commit to them, and link them to reflective practices*. The insights we gain establish the foundation for our personal and professional development practice.

We may regard these tools are mere activities or a way to pass the time. Please do not make that mistake. Instead, trust that how we spend our time, how we choose to ground ourselves provides a frame for and influences how we observe, filter information, make decisions, and find meaning in our lives.

Sometime soon, maybe even today, we'll meet someone who disrupts our plans and unsettles our emotions. When this happens, consider the ideas laid out here as potential instructions for learning how to drive results through others more effectively. Managing the minor inconveniences and major stumbling blocks of daily life with less conflict is something we must learn, and practice.

This little guide enables us with all the tools and tactics we need to make our interactions less stressful and more effective.

5 Principles For Driving Results With Others

In 1995, author and science journalist Daniel Goleman wrote *Emotional Intelligence: Why It Can Matter More Than IQ*. The book was groundbreaking but remained on the fringe of business literature for several decades. Emotional intelligence is the capacity to be aware of, control, and express one's emotions, and to handle interpersonal relationships judiciously and empathetically. Today, the concept of emotional intelligence is widely accepted as the practical application of an individual's ability to apply their knowledge of emotions to manage their own behavior and to influence others.

Goleman suggested that emotional intelligence is as important as intellect when considering an individual's success. He went on to state that emotional intelligence is a skill that can be taught and outlined a method for incorporating emotional skills using five key principles.

1. **Increase self-awareness.**

   Awareness is about learning to know what you know and feel what you feel. Sounds simple, but when we deny or

are in conflict with our thoughts and feelings, a kind of
"social static" increases when we attempt to connect with
others. People who are comfortable with their own thoughts
and feelings have a greater capacity for understanding how
they impact others. They connect with others in a way that
increases their effectiveness.

2. **Learn to self-regulate.**

   Control and manage our impulses and emotions. Reacting instead of responding can lead to mistakes, less critical
   thinking, and can often damage relationships.

3. **Cultivate empathy.**

   Understanding our own emotions is only half of the work
   in a conversation. Learning how to constructively understand and respond to the emotions of others is also critical
   to our effectiveness working with others: observe specific
   behaviors; be curious about the mood or emotion from
   another person; and, find a way to connect with them.
   Empathy helps develop our relationships.

4. **Understand your own motivation.**

   There is no direct line to happiness from external definitions
   of success, like money, titles, rank, and material rewards.
   Having a sense of mission, passion, or fascination with what
   we do leads to sustained attachment and motivation with our
   work. Strong motivation increases clarity of decision making
   and priorities.

5. **Develop social skills.**

   Social skills are more than just being friendly or, as some
   more resistant to the EQ message put it "being kinder and
   gentler". Goleman describes social skills as "friendliness
   with a purpose." We are polite and respectful, and also *intentional.* Healthy relationships can be used for personal and
   organizational benefit; they can help us advance, develop
   others, and get things done.

How to Use this Book

Simple chapter headings are organized by Goleman's key principles: self-awareness, self-regulation, empathy, motivation, and social skills.

Each chapter starts with three key components:

Questions Common questions we experience when attempting to drive results through others.

Responses Responses to consider reframing a challenging experience.

Quotes Sometimes others say it best. Quotes from leaders to inspire and help cultivate new perspectives.

A single idea is discussed, followed by several helpful reinforcements:

Panel of Masters Other perspectives to help you develop a roundtable of advice-givers.

Remember A succinct chapter summary or helpful soundbite, to help reinforce your learning.

Practice Apply your learning by digging into your experience and testing your knowledge.

Connect Seek and nurture a panel of peers, bosses, mentors for advice and feedback. We learn most with and through others.

Reflect Engage the prompts for a reflective practice, return to those that help you most. Over time, it's also very helpful data and record of progress.

This table appears at the end of the book where you will be able to build your own practice for driving results through others.

#	TOPIC TITLES	SELF-AWARENESS	SELF-REGULATION	EMPATHY	MOTIVATION	SOCIAL SKILLS	PAGE
1	Opportunities Are Everywhere.	●					27
2	Emotions Teach Us.	●					33
3	Cultivate Perspective.	●					39
4	Using Challenge To Grow.	●					45
5	Be Your Own Guide.	●					53
6	You Are In Control.		●				61
7	Maintain Inner Peace.		●				67
8	Emotions Are Contagious.		●				73
9	Anger Means Danger.		●				81
10	Go Beyond Worry.		●				87
11	Be Compassionate.			●			95
12	Find Patience.			●			101
13	Learn From Everyone, Even Them.			●			107
14	Check Your Filters.			●			115
15	Ask More Questions.			●			121
16	Find Stamina.				●		129
17	Know Your Motivations.				●		137
18	Develop A Practice.				●		143
19	Focus On The Small.				●		149
20	Hold Tension.				●		155
21	Don't Compromise…Yourself.					●	163
22	Build Bonds.					●	169
23	Persuade.					●	175
24	Cooperate.					●	181
25	Embrace Emotional Labor.					●	189

Be Creative. Be Intentional

Use this pocket guide to stimulate your own reflection process.

- **Flip and Find**

  For help in the moment, scan the chapter question/answers for an issue you are experiencing in the moment. Gain an alternative perspective.

- **Pause & Practice**

  Use the prompts as inspiration for your own practice. Make note of particular prompts, quotes, questions, or suggestions that resonate by checking the box at the end of each chapter.

- **Rinse & Repeat**

  Return to prompts you've checked to develop and deepen your practice. This is how strength in your performance is developed.

1

Increase Self Awareness

Awareness is about learning to know what we know and feel what we feel. Learn to decrease "social static" by connecting with others in a way that increases our effectiveness.

- **Opportunities are everywhere.** Because we will cross paths with people who challenge our thoughts and reactions our whole lives, it's important to learn how to work with them sooner rather than later. They teach us about ourselves and challenge us to be better people. We can take comfort in the fact that, with the right tools and strategies, we can learn to deal with personalities and circumstances that challenge us in ways that are constructive and help move us and others forward.

- **Emotions teach us.** How we respond to another person is a direct reflection of our skill level in working with and through others. If we can gain awareness of our reactivity, we can gain focus on what to improve.

- **Cultivate perspective.** The hurt feelings that come from remembering how we were slighted can run deep and have physiological and emotional impacts on us. When we feel intensity, it's important to step back and cultivate perspective.

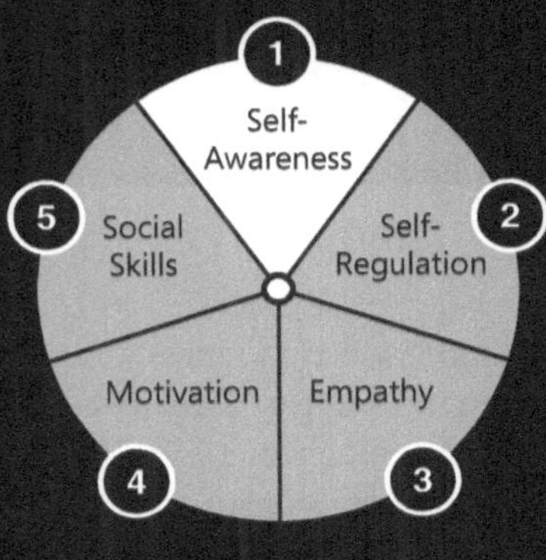

There are many practices to consider aiding the skill of cultivating attention.

- **Find traction.** There are no dead ends. Tipping back or becoming stuck teaches valuable lessons about how to get back on track. Focusing our attention allows us to accumulate small wins. Framing our views determines our direction. Amplifying what works increases our momentum and ultimately gets us back on track.

- **Be your own guide.** To cope with momentary stress or that of larger goals, commit to a practice. Investing in developing muscle memory pays off in better performance and smarter choices under pressure. Practice helps you process much of the "static of life" with greater skill.

I'm finding new ways to mess up on lessons I thought I had learned from past experience. It's like I'm finding challenge and change wherever I turn. Why do I seem to encounter so many challenging situations?

First, many people find themselves relearning old lessons when presented in new contexts. When an experience we think we know is camouflaged, it's harder to spot.

Second, there's no easy answer as to why you feel you are encountering more challenge at this particular time. Regardless, you play a role in whatever dynamic you are in so it's worth examining. There might be another way to perceive what you are experiencing. Understanding alternative perspectives can create opportunities for alternative approaches to connect and collaborate more effectively.

"The best laid schemes o' mice an' men
Gang aft a-gley, [often go awry]"

–ROBERT BURNS,
Scottish poet and lyricist

There are times we learn a lesson and we think it will stick. We increase our vigilance and sensitivity to certain circumstances, or personalities. "We will never do that again!", we say to ourselves— only to turn around and do it again. Nature abhors a void.

When we find ourselves learning the same lesson over and over, we never really learned the lesson completely in the first place. For instance, a domineering parent can consciously or unconsciously attract us to overbearing life partners or bosses. We learned that lesson in the family context, but when we encountered similar dynamics in the workplace, we didn't catch on until it was too late.

Personal dynamics are the single most important variable to every project we undertake. We cannot ignore how we and those around us confront challenge and change.

Reality doesn't always measure up to our aspirations. We can think through plans and strategies all day, but once we include others into the equation we need to adapt, often. Why? Because we must interact as fluidly as possible with people from every social class, rank, profession, and institution to overcome obstacles and drive results.

People will show up, sometimes out of the blue, asking contro-versial questions, interjecting feedback late in the game, and requiring us to accommodate their needs before our own. They will ignore the positives, and focus on the negatives. They make us experience a range of unconstructive emotions—unease, anger, fear, anxiety, frustration—just to name a few. These individuals can show up in a hurry and leave our lives just as quickly. But sometimes they stick around, becoming permanent fixtures, and we can't escape them.

What do we do about people that inhabit our lives and invade our emotional space? First, we should regard them as our best teachers. Every chance we connect with challenge is an opportunity to learn something about how we operate and can operate more effectively. They highlight our potential for deeper virtues, helping us work on our patience, grit, and courage.

Often, those that antagonize us teach us lessons we would have no other way of learning. Adversity is the path toward growth.

Learning to navigate challenging interpersonal relationships without compromising our ethics or personal values is the goal. So instead of worrying about the fact that we will eventually have to work through others to drive results, we must open up to the possibility of learning more about ourselves. Listen for the lessons. As we gain more self-awareness about how we operate, we'll become more effective at what we do, creating more possibilities, better results, and deeper connections.

Generally speaking, we have three levels of awareness:

1. Initial awareness is gained through reflection after an incident occurs. If we understand what the gap in our behavior is and know what it should be, we have a shot at catching ourselves in the act the next time.

2. When we successfully catch ourselves in the moment, we get just enough time to make a different choice.

3. When we catch ourselves enough times, we can spot a trigger coming rather than having it blindside us into rash reactivity. Seeing a trigger coming gives us even more time to choose a different reaction.

> NOTE: We are in and out of these three phases all the time based on how snagged we are at any time and how aware we are of our triggers when we are snagged by people or circumstances that challenge us.

"We are all fallen creatures and
all very hard to live with."
— C.S. Lewis,
British writer and lay theologian

"Difficult people are the greatest teachers."
— Pema Chödrön,
American Tibetan Buddhist nun

"We are all human and fall short of where we
need to be. We must never stop trying
to be the best we can be."
— Richard Adams,
English novelist and writer

"The awareness that we are all human beings
together has become lost in war
and through politics."
— Albert Schweitzer,
Alsatian polymath, theologian, writer, and physician

 Because we will cross paths with people who challenge our thoughts and reactions our whole lives, it's important to learn how to work with them sooner rather than later. They teach us about ourselves and challenge us to be better people. We can take comfort in the fact that, with the right tools and strategies, we can learn to deal with personalities and circumstances that challenge us in ways that are constructive and help move us and others forward.

 Consider several recent situations in which you have crossed paths with challenging personalities. What feelings came up? What thoughts did you have that turned into beliefs about how people operate? Can those beliefs be broadened? How did you ultimately deal with them? How could you have handled things differently?

 Talk to a friend or trusted colleague about ways in which you've dealt with people who challenge you. Consider several alternatives to these actions for dealing with them in the future. Having alternatives at the ready for next time increases your ability to be creative in the moment.

If you keep a journal for your own development, write down the ways that you typically respond to people with challenging personalities.

What are the positive aspects of your typical response?

____

____

____

____

____

What are the negative aspects?

____

____

____

____

____

If you'd like to continue thinking about this idea in the future, check the box

At the end of the book, you can summarize all the practices that worked for you and start to generate your own curriculum.

It seems like I've still got a long way to go, so much to still learn, about working through others. When I feel like I don't know what I'm doing, where do I start?

There will always be more to learn, new ways of communicating and connecting with people. And, what got you here is not what will get you to the next level. When you find that old skills aren't working, it means it's time to learn a new one that will give you deeper insights and help you navigate other relationships too.

"A man cannot be comfortable
without his own approval."

— Mark Twain,
American writer and lecturer

""My scope doubled; I don't know how to address a team, an organization, or a company that large!"

"I just got promoted to group lead, director, or general manager—and I feel like I don't know what I'm doing."

"I need to deliver some challenging feedback, and I'm scared I'll do it wrong."

Everyone—from the CEO to the intern—learns on the job. When we learn in front of others, when the stakes are high—uncertainty, anger, anxiety, frustration—can show up like unwanted guests. How we manage our feelings in these situations determines how we will engage with others, and it is a direct reflection on our skill level in working effectively through them.

In situations that are new to us, we often find others to be the problem. We might perceive everyone else to be more difficult than usual. That might be an indicator that we need to improve our own skills. We might need to get better at contracting, negotiating, influencing, dealing with resistance, managing others, delivering feedback, influencing without authority, influencing with authority, communicating the right message at the right time, or just meeting the other person's needs in the moment.

Slowing down to gain a broader perspective—one beyond our own immediate reactivity—can expose our idiosyncrasies, quirks, and vulnerabilities. If we pay attention to how we react to different kinds of personalities, we can learn better ways to *respond*.

When it comes to learning, we can take the easy way or the hard way. For many of us, the list of easily learned lessons is pretty short.

As individuals, we want to grow intellectually, spiritually, *and* emotionally. The issue might be that, if we're really honest, we don't equally value those three qualities. This results in us having lopsided skills. Regardless of what the organizational tolerance for drama is, if we value technical expertise or bottom-line results more than we value managing and developing others, we will likely be less influential than our peers.

When we resist learning in any one of these categories, we are still being taught—whether we like it or not! Seats are always open in the School of Hard Knocks.

"Human beings, who are almost unique in having
the ability to learn from the experience
of others, are also remarkable for their
apparent disinclination to do so."
— Douglas Adams,
English author, Hitchhiker's Guide to the Galaxy

"You should never try to be better than someone
else, you should always be learning from others.
But you should never cease trying to be the best
you could be because that's under your control
and the other isn't."
— John Wooden,
American basketball player and head coach at UCLA

"Example is not the main thing in influencing
others. It is the only thing."
— Albert Schweitzer,
polymath, theologian, writer, philosopher, and physician

"Learning from other people
is what music is all about."
— Neil Young,
Canadian singer-songwriter

How we respond to another person is a direct reflection of our skill level in working with and through others. If we can gain awareness of our reactivity, we can gain focus on what to improve.

Think back to the last time you felt overwhelmed by responsibility or lacked the right skills. Remember the feeling(s) you had at the time and name them. Name the skills you felt you lacked at the time. Now think back to the people you were working with, in particular, those you experienced as challenging. What lesson did you learn from them? How did that lesson contribute to your personal or professional development?

Talk to a friend or trusted colleague about the ways in which you both have matured during the last few years. How has challenge and change taught you lessons you couldn't have learned from other, more easygoing people?

If you keep a journal for your own development, write down your thoughts about the joys and rewards of being a lifelong learner.

____

____

____

____

____

____

Are there any negative aspects of lifelong learning?

____

____

____

____

____

If you'd like to continue thinking about this idea in the future, check the box

At the end of the book, you can summarize all the practices that worked for you and start to generate your own curriculum.

There are people who have slighted me over the years, and I find myself carrying grudges. How can I let those go?

Wounds sting, making it hard to move on from the slings and arrows. To say "forgiveness is its own reward" falls flat when retribution is closer at hand. Because feelings can run deep, there are several answers to consider: find patience, don't hold grudges, go beyond worry, and…it's important to cultivate perspective.

"Everything that irritates us about others
can lead us to an understanding of ourselves."

— CARL JUNG,
Swiss psychiatrist and psychoanalyst

When we experience stress, our bodies release a chemical cocktail that impacts how we take in information. People might withhold information, cut you from important meetings, or hold back on their contributions to our work—that behavior can have a direct impact on our ability to do our job and the trajectory of our career. Challenge can be a threat or opportunity. How we confront challenge can tip us forward or backward in our performance.

When we carry grudges, we are holding on to emotions that release naturally occurring hormones which amplify and distort our perspective. They may amplify thoughts of "everyone hates me," or "they are against me" when in fact most people aren't giving us much thought because they are living their own dramas. When we feel slighted or "done to" we are less likely to filter the meaningful from the mundane.

Our nerves might feel raw. Our energy is generally lower. We oscillate between feeling wildly unfocused or having tunnel vision.

Grudges—how long we hold on to them, why we choose to cling to them—are tied to stories we tell about ourselves. Who we think we are and what we think we deserve or are entitled to is a matter of perception. What makes one person feel slighted might not impact someone else the same way.

Instead of thinking of concentrating on how you felt slighted, how can you view the person or situation through another pair of eyes? How can you learn to view them differently? Can you try to see the situation differently? what will it take to get you to more neutral territory?

Who knows, the other person might be under tremendous pressures at home or might not know how they are impacting you. They might be struggling in their role and feel like they don't know what they're doing. Can you relate to that feeling?

There isn't one person out there today that couldn't stand to gain from the benefit of the doubt.

Find ways of cultivating perspective by trying different practices. For example, learn the differences between:

Attention. Attention is what we are focusing on in the moment. Attention is limited, selective, and a very basic component of our biological makeup.

Meta-Attention. Meta-attention is attention of attention. A shorthand way of thinking of it is a balcony view of a situation. It is, *what we think and how we feel* about what we are noticing. The ability to pay attention to attention itself raises our cognitive functioning and enables response over reactivity. For example, when we become bored, our attention wanders. Sometimes something clicks and we are reminded we need to be paying attention. We can catch ourselves and bring our attention back to the task at hand.

Meta-attention is the key to deep concentration and awareness. When our meta-attention becomes strong, we can keep our wandering mind on task. Rather than long periods of boredom of fidgeting, we can recover our attention quickly and often enough to experience continuity of our own experience, a more continuous attention, which is deep concentration.

Meditation. Meditation is about mental training practices. The goal is to distinguish between two specific mental process: Attention and Meta-attention.

Mindfulness. Mindfulness is a quality of being — the experience of being open and aware in the present moment, without reflexive judgment, automatic criticism or mind wandering.

"To be wronged is nothing,
unless you continue to remember it."

— CONFUCIUS,
Chinese philosopher and politician

"There are no facts,
only interpretations."

— FRIEDRICH NIETZSCHE,
German philosopher

"One person's craziness
is another person's reality."

— TIM BURTON,
American filmmaker

"It's the hardest thing in the world
to go on being aware of
someone else's pain."

— PAT BARKER,
English writer and novelist

 The hurt feelings that come from remembering how we were slighted can run deep and have physiological and emotional impacts on us. When we feel intensity, it's important to step back and cultivate perspective. There are many practices to consider aiding the skill of cultivating attention.

 Make a list of the people you judge harshly and/or have the need to forgive. It could be for small things like ghosting you, making promises and not keeping them, professional slights, reputational damage—anything. Consider why these behaviors have a hold on you, and what you need to gain a better perspective in order to move on.

 Talk to a friend or trusted colleague about how you have gained perspective in the past. Consider a time when you took a trip, journaled, engaged a coach or therapist, focused on a hobby, made some kind of change in your life that shifted your perspective.

If you keep a journal for your own development, list
the small shifts you would like to integrate to shift
your perspective.

____

____

____

____

____

____

____

____

____

____

If you'd like to continue thinking about this idea in the future,
check the box

At the end of the book, you can summarize all the practices
that worked for you and start to generate your own curriculum.

I don't want to be stuck. I want to keep learning and developing. How do I get out of my own way?

Maturity is an ongoing journey, not a final destination. This truth is something we often need to learn and relearn in multiple contexts to truly understand and integrate into our lives. Tipping back after accomplishing something big is normal. Plateauing is normal. *The key is to maintain forward momentum overall.*

To do so, you have to find tools and strategies that help you move forward by challenging you and moving you past your comfort zone. And, you have to be *deliberate about practicing* those tools and strategies your whole life. Stuckness happens when we take our achievements and the practices that got us there for granted.

Maturity requires a certain amount of discomfort, of varying degrees, ongoing. Maturing is a *process*, not a state.

"There is a tendency at every important
but difficult crossroad to pretend
that it's not really there."

— CARL JUNG,
Swiss psychiatrist and psychoanalyst

No mud, no lotus. It's as simple as that. We understand this idea intellectually, but not so much in practice.

How do we gain awareness of the slight shifts in our behavior between the achievement of a goal and being stuck trying to maintain it? The challenge of achievement is much, much different than the challenge of maintenance. Think of the last time you tried to get in shape, versus what it took to stay in shape. Being stuck infers, to some degree, that we got somewhere, but we can no longer move elsewhere. The challenge, that hill we are after, might not be as clear to us.

Was location the problem, do we feel like we are buried under a rock? Are resources the issue, do we not have enough to sustain our efforts? Are the conditions right, do we have the appropriate environment to nurture our growth? Are we stuck in the past, do we operate under old paradigms when things around us have shifted? Are our goals still appropriate?

Did we abandon our goals after we achieved them? Did we take our accomplishments for granted? Did we forget how hard it was to achieve? Did we watch them slowly erode?

When we feel stuck, deep in the mud, we feel restricted, hampered, hamstrung, beleaguered, depressed, myopic, frustrated, behind, out of synch, resentful, tired, angry—and any number of painful feelings. Pain builds. This happens to people as well as organizations.

When we get our cars stuck in the mud, *traction is required to get us unstuck*. For a big, heavy car all it takes is a bag of cat litter and some sticks. At the end of the day, we won't shift gears until we are sick of whatever is causing us to be stuck.

How can we focus, frame, and amplify that pain in a way that enables traction?

- **Focus.** Start small. Find and accumulate small wins. Having ploughed this ground already makes us the expert on how to avoid the landmines.

- **Frame.** Cut through the overwhelm of pain to spot patterns in the chaos. We achieved, we tipped back. What brought us here? Along the way, where did our priorities shift? One frame to consider is: there are no dead ends. Tipping back or being stuck has taught us a valuable lesson: what is it? What will it take to have the glass half full again? How we frame our views, determines our direction.

- **Amplify.** After starting small and directing our views, we need to amplify what is working. Leaning more and more into that direction is what will help build momentum.

"You should never view your challenges as a disadvantage. Instead, it's important for you to understand that your experience facing and overcoming adversity is actually one of your biggest advantages."
— MICHELLE OBAMA,
American lawyer, university administrator, writer, and former first lady of the United States

"I think we're going to the moon because it's in the nature of the human being to face challenges. It's by the nature of his deep inner soul... we're required to do these things just as salmon swim upstream."
— NEIL ARMSTRONG,
American astronaut and aeronautical engineer and the first person to walk on the Moon

"Optimistic people play a disproportionate role in shaping our lives. Their decisions make a difference; they are inventors, entrepreneurs, political and military leaders - not average people. They got to where they are by seeking challenges and taking risks."
— DANIEL KAHNEMAN,
Israeli-American psychologist and economist

 There are no dead ends. Tipping back or being stuck teaches valuable lessons about how to get back on track. Framing our views determines our direction. Amplifying what works increases our momentum and ultimately gets us back on track.

 Think back to a time you achieved a goal but later felt stuck. What behaviors tipped you back toward being stuck? What behaviors tipped your forward toward gaining traction?

 Talk to a friend or trusted colleague about times when you needed to find traction. What was the particular traction you found? How did you focus, frame and amplify it?

If you keep a journal for your own development,
reflect on a situation when you were stuck. What was
one thing going right at the time?

____

____

____

____

____

____

How did you gain enough traction to get unstuck?

____

____

____

____

____

If you'd like to continue thinking about this idea in the future,
check the box

At the end of the book, you can summarize all the practices
that worked for you and start to generate your own curriculum.

There are times when I get overwhelmed by everything coming at me, and I just want someone to tell me what to do. There's too much information. I get stuck in the overwhelm and can't find my way.

When you have too much input coming at you, you must recognize that it is temporary.

Under pressure, it is what you practice most that will inform the actions you take. If that is panic, you panic. If that is finding ways to gain perspective, you start looking for the anchors.

"No man is great enough or wise enough
for any of us to surrender our destiny
to. The only way in which anyone can
lead us is to restore to us the belief in
our own guidance."

— HENRY MILLER,
American writer

When confronted with the initial jitters of change—reorganization, downsizing, losing a client, a new relationship, a second career, a change in scope—our first thoughts are never our fault. We might feel uncertain, unworthy, like an imposter, scared, frustrated, resentful, and even excited. Sensations, feelings, and thoughts run through us when we experience stress of any kind.

First, we process stress *physically*. We seldom listen to our bodies, but we have a powerful instrument giving us data all the time. Pay attention to physical sensations: jitters, butterflies, nausea, panic, sweat, irregular breathing, or tightness in neck, back, etc.

Second, our feelings are amplified. The tightness in our neck and the frustration we feel in this moment, *emotionally* we are kicking into high gear.

Then, our minds race as we process thoughts *intellectually*. How do we have so many thoughts, so quickly? Our physical, emotional and intellectual state has made us flinch and focus, very narrowly. With this tunnel-vision, we select data in these moments of stress, data that might not serve us in taking the best action. From this data we make assumptions. These assumptions inform conclusions. Our conclusions evolve into (perhaps, misguided) beliefs. Those beliefs inform the choices we make.

Ultimately, when we experience stress, we "believe" we start with the feeling, in this case, overwhelm. This is how we emotionally experience stress. But we bypassed our physical sensations. We actually went through several physical sensations first. Then our minds raced with thoughts, assumptions, conclusions, and beliefs before arriving at feeling overwhelmed. And it all happened in less than 3 seconds!

Physical sensations, a rush of emotions, and a deluge of thoughts are three signs that we might be jumping to an incorrect conclusion. In the midst of this flurry, being your own guide is about finding ways to create stillness within.

A compassionate and understanding response to this behavior is to understand that our first thoughts are never our fault. They are a function of our defense mechanisms, which are years in the making. Our next thoughts, however, are up to us.

Everyone needs techniques to help define their goals and maintain momentum. This is as true for experiencing stress in a single moment as it is for larger life goals. Without deliberate practice, development can take years of trial and error. Accelerate your personal and professional transformation by cultivating a practice of self-reflection. Use the guides and prompts in this book as a start. Incorporate small experiments into your day-to-day.

"If you follow the voice inside you,
it does give you guidance."
— GLORIA STEINEM,
American feminist, journalist, and social political activist

"Your automatic guidance system
cannot guide you when you're standing still."
— MAXWELL MALTZ,
American cosmetic surgeon and author

"Nothing is impossible when we follow our inner
guidance, even when its direction may threaten us
by reversing our usual logic."
— GERALD JAMPOLSKY,
American author

"You have to become very still and listen while your
inner voice—the very essence of you—tells you who
you are. You'll know you've found it when every cell in
your body practically vibrates; when you're filled up by
what you're doing instead of being drained by it."
— OPRAH WINFREY,
American media executive, actress, and philanthropist

 To cope with momentary stress or that of larger goals, commit to a practice. Investing in developing muscle memory pays off in better performance and smarter choices under pressure. Practice helps you process much of the "static of life" with greater skill.

 If guidance is what you are looking for, look within, first. The questions you ask, and how you ask them directs the way you think:

- **Momentary goals:** *How can I handle overwhelm?* Stop. Observe your sensations, feelings and thoughts. Question your assumptions, conclusions, and beliefs.

- **Larger goals:** *Am I ready for a promotion?* What will it take to get promoted? Get past the "checklist" of skills required and start looking at your temperament and ability to work with others. As you move up content knowledge is assumed. Measurement of trust, transparency, rapport are all subjective and matter more.

 Talk to a friend or trusted colleague about specific ways in which you can learn to be a better guide to yourself. Seek opinions from others about how you show up in different scenarios. Feedback from mentors, coaches, or trusted colleagues provides additional perspective on what you can work on to be more effective.

If you keep a journal for your own development, write your thoughts about what "voice" speaks to you at times you need direction. What tone is it using and what is it saying?

____

____

____

____

How did you learn from missteps?

____

____

____

____

What skills do you wish to learn in the future?

____

____

____

____

If you'd like to continue thinking about this idea in the future, check the box

At the end of the book, you can summarize all the practices that worked for you and start to generate your own curriculum.

2

Increase Self-Regulation

Self-regulation helps us Control and manage our impulses and emotions. Reacting instead of responding can lead to mistakes, less critical thinking, and can often damage relationships.

- **You are in control.** You have more in control over yourself and your circumstances than you think. If you're dealing with the difficulties of challenge and change, remember that you have tools and strategies of your practice (faith, reflection, meditation, simple breathing, naming your feeling, choosing alternative responses) you can rely upon.

- **Maintain inner peace.** Inner peace is a resource that is always available to us, even under the most intense life pressures. Patience is a quality of emotional equilibrium—and to develop, it requires constant practice. Our aim is to find a neutral equilibrium. Neutrality is where we enjoy the highest creativity, where we see the most alternatives to instant reactivity.

- **Emotions are contagious.** Emotions are contagious. When we're in the presence of people who challenge us, we are more likely to take on some aspect of their emotional state. Anxiety, like the flu, likes to travel. However, if we are mentally prepared, we can create enough psychological distance to

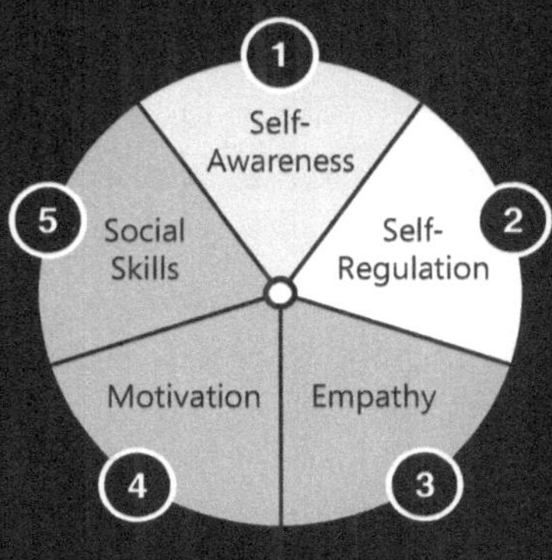

remain calm and neutral in the presence of volatility. Call out what is happening. Get curious about why the other person (or we) feel a certain way. State the goal (or request help) and move on.

- **Anger means danger.** When furious, get curious. If you think you are about to lose your patience because you are some shade of angry (frustrated, irritated or annoyed)—take a beat, slow down and turn the attention onto yourself.

- **Go beyond worry.** We have worries. We also have solutions. Our challenge is to trust that we can solve a problem with creativity and considered response instead of reactivity.

 Wherever I turn, I experience challenge. Why does this happen?

 Depending on how we show up in life, or the role that we play in whatever groups we find ourselves in, we attract certain personalities. Learning we have some influence over this can help us mitigate that attraction.

 "The best indicator of your level of consciousness is how you deal with life's challenges when they come. Through those challenges, an already unconscious person tends to become more deeply unconscious, and a conscious person more intensely conscious. You can use a challenge to awaken you, or you can allow it to pull you into even deeper sleep. The dream of ordinary unconsciousness then turns into a nightmare."

— ECKHART TOLLE,
German-Canadian author

Why do some people encounter more challenge with change than others? Two common reasons are perception and situational role.

Some people have a mental model that challenge and change are threatening. Other people viewing the very same set of circumstances might experience opportunity. There is ample research and marketing for both perspectives. Ultimately our mental models come from our lived experience. Regardless of our individual bias of change and challenge, everyone in an organization needs to understand change brings an energy force that requires management and direction. Ideas from the outside can be necessary bacteria to help germinate new solutions. They can also be toxic viruses that could kill what's working. Either way, adaptation is what keeps organizations vital and relevant. Resistance stands alongside the gatekeeper of all this change, seeking to preserve status quo. Preservatives prolong the shelf-life of ideas, processes, standards, mechanisms, and scaffolding for what works (and sometimes what doesn't).

Whether we are bringing ideas in, casting them out, adapting them to fit, or preserving them, our roles leading change put us at the forefront of challenge and change. Perhaps we prefer the company of people who buck change because we see it as a form of resisting unnecessary authority. Or, maybe we have experienced challenging personalities in our family and because that is what is familiar to us, we gravitate toward those qualities in others—consciously or unconsciously. For example, we might perceive people who challenge others and bring change to be honest and upfront about their agenda.

Regardless of how we reason with challenge and change, there is some level of individual agency we have to learn in order to drive results with others. When confronted with difficulty, our challenge is to trust, listen, and learn—about *ourselves* and others.

The next time we encounter some bumpy road, we can't give in to anxiety, worrying or complaining. Instead, our task is to stay calm and ground ourselves. Before we react, we need to give ourselves enough emotional distance to generate alternative responses. When we see other choices, we generally try them. The emotional storm will pass, probably sooner than you think. Emotions are a lot like the weather; they are temporary.

"Change yourself - you are in control."

— Mahatma Gandhi,
Indian lawyer, anti-colonial nationalist, and political ethicist

"Imagine that you are in control of your life.
Now, the question is:
Why do you have to imagine this?"

— Ernie J Zelinski,
American author

"Only you can control your future."

— Theodor Seuss Geisel,
American children's author, political cartoonist, illustrator

"All of a sudden
you realize that you are the person
who has control of your life."

— Jim Henson,
American puppeteer, animator, cartoonist, actor, inventor,
filmmaker, and screenwriter

You have more control over yourself and your circumstances than you think. If you're dealing with the difficulties of challenge and change, remember that you have tools and strategies of your practice (faith, reflection, meditation, simple breathing, naming your feeling, choosing alternative responses) you can rely upon.

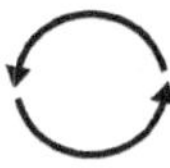

The next time you cross paths with challenge and change remind yourself that it is a learning moment. What is it you notice most about your own reactivity during these encounters? How can you be more curious about the bodily sensations (tightness, sweating, breathing), feelings (frustration, etc.), or thoughts you are having? What thoughts are you clinging to? There is something valuable in that moment designed to move you forward.

Talk to a friend or trusted colleague about the lessons you both can learn when confronted with a challenge. What more do you notice now that you did not at the time?

If you keep a journal for your own development, write down thoughts about how others influence your everyday life, positive or negative. What specific, observable behavior do they have?

____

____

____

____

____

Watch for how many judgmental terms come to mind, and how hard it is to get to the kind of behaviors you can observe only with your eyes. What attracts you or repels you about how others operate?

____

____

____

____

If you'd like to continue thinking about this idea in the future, check the box

At the end of the book, you can summarize all the practices that worked for you and start to generate your own curriculum.

When I'm confronted with a challenging person or situation, I feel robbed of my inner peace. How can I remain grounded?

Inner peace is a quality we seek in faith, meditation, yoga, exercise, or any deep hobby where we can deeply focus. Challenge—whether we encounter it in others or situations—disrupts the kind of focus that grounds us, leaving us unsettled. The key is to be able to ground yourself wherever you are, in whatever circumstances you find yourself.

"Inner peace begins the moment you choose
not to allow another person or event
to control your emotions."

— PEMA CHODRON,
American Tibetan Buddhist nun

Thomas Boyce, a developmental pediatrician working with troubled children, explored how genetic make-up and environment shape behavior. He uses the metaphor of a "dandelion" child (hardy, resilient, healthy), able to survive and flourish under most circumstances, and the "orchid" child (sensitive, susceptible, fragile), who, given the right support, can thrive as much as, if not more than, other children.

So, when we're unsettled, which flower are we, the dandelion or the orchid? It can be hard to be remain grounded when we are confronted by challenge and change. For example, if we experience someone we are working with to be under-performing, it's hard to be curious and understand why that may be happening. It might be harder still to think we might play any part in their performance. But what if we are contributing to their downward journey? Wouldn't we want to know how to be and do better (for both our sakes)?

We're human, and we fall short. We get easily irritated. We can be quick to judge. We allow ourselves to get easily frustrated by others' shortcomings even though we show remarkable tolerance with our own. We are imperfect people in an imperfect world. We have imperfect parents, elect to be with imperfect partners, work for imperfect bosses, mix with imperfect colleagues, and have imperfect friends. Sometimes we inherit troubles from imperfect people. Sometimes we create imperfect situations all on our own. In either case, patience helps. We have to find patience for others' shortcomings as well as our own.

For most of us, when we find ourselves under pressure, patience is hard to summon, let alone curiosity. We'd rather give in to the release that irritation or frustration offer because it makes us feel better, if only temporarily. The chemical epinephrine is rapidly produced by the adrenal gland when a person experiences frustration, anger, or other forms of stress. When we are challenged or under pressure, we want a release from that feeling. We want action—fight or flight. Something. Anything.

Patience is a quality of emotional equilibrium—and to develop, it requires constant practice. Our aim is always to find an *equilibrium*. Neutrality is where we enjoy the highest creativity, where we see the most alternatives to instant reactivity. It is the state of mind where time slows down, where we have the emotional distance and perspective to think to ourselves, "I could have tried…" "Next time I might try…."

Sometimes frustration can help lead us to a helpful shift in strategy. When we find we are spending too long trying to crack a bad nut, our survival demands we move on to another one. Frustration can also lead us astray and destroy persistence. Patience helps determine the best decision.

"You find peace not by rearranging the circumstances of your life, but by realizing who you are at the deepest level."

— ECKHART TOLLE,
German author

"If there is to be any peace it will come through being, not having."

— HENRY MILLER,
American author and playwright

"Meditation is not a way of making your mind quiet. It is a way of entering into the quiet that is already there – buried under the 50,000 thoughts the average person thinks every day."

— DEEPAK CHOPRA,
American author

"The nearer a man comes to a calm mind, the closer he is to strength."

— MARCUS AURELIUS,
Roman emperor and Stoic philosopher

 Inner peace is a resource that is always available to us, even under the most intense life pressures. Patience is a quality of emotional equilibrium—and to develop, it requires constant practice. Our aim is to find an *emotional equilibrium*. Neutrality is where we enjoy the highest creativity, where we see the most alternatives to instant reactivity.

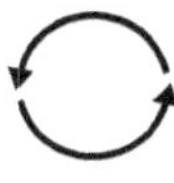 When we're confronted by people who challenge us or situations we find stressful, it is hard to remain grounded. Challenge yourself to think through the last hour. How many interactions did you enter with a mind for peace?

 Talk to a friend or trusted colleague about how each interaction we have is about either perpetuating the idea of peace or disrupting it.

If you keep a journal for your own development, write down your thoughts about the ways you can find peace and keep it. If that feels out of reach, remember the last time you felt peaceful, and what contributed to that feeling.

____

____

____

____

____

____

____

____

____

____

If you'd like to continue thinking about this idea in the future, check the box

At the end of the book, you can summarize all the practices that worked for you and start to generate your own curriculum.

When I'm confronted with challenge and change, my emotions seem to fluctuate—and they get away from me. I hear about a re-organization, I wonder what will happen to my role. I don't hear back from my boss right away, I think they aren't impressed with my performance. I'm more reactionary than I normally am. How can I get a handle on this?

Emotions are like the flu. Sometimes you can "catch" them from other people. When people around us are emotionally distressed we might be tempted to become upset too. We need to maintain a safe Psychological distance, where their problems are not our problems.

"We don't want to be afraid to make a choice
because we're afraid to make a mistake.
Decisions aren't final. Feelings change all
the time. Taking risks and making
choices are what make life so exciting.
Every day something new
comes our way.
"

— AMY POEHLER,
American actress, comedian, director,
producer, and writer

Many of us find the value of reflection through faith, meditation, physical workouts, hobbies, or other centering activity. Yet, try as we might, negative feelings can rob us of our *emotional equilibrium*. It sounds counterintuitive, but neutrality is where we are most grounded and creative. From neutral, we see the full range of possibilities. One side calls us to anger, irritation, frustration, impatience, or anxiety has the power to detach us from our goals. The other side invites us to ride a wave of euphoria, joy, victory, and kinship potentially eclipsing important data from our view. From neutral, we can connect more deeply and develop the *feel* for the work at hand, placing aside thefeelings that will lead us astray. We can stand our ground in the presence of a bully. We can influence an unaligned stakeholder, or have a hard conversation with a teammember about their performance.

Separating feelings from feel is hardest when we are under pressure to perform well. From first-time manager to CEO, we learn on the job. We lead companies, delegate as a newly minted director, manage through others, facilitate small groups and speak to large groups—all through some form of trial and error.

Emotions are contagious. Ever been able to avoid smiling around a laughing baby? Recall how uplifting it is to be around genuinely positive people?

In the workplace, we tend to focus on the negative emotions we need to contain or manage. For instance, when we must have a hard conversation with a colleague. If the other person is aware this conversation is coming, they might be nervous. We might be nervous approaching them, hoping it will go well. They sense us, we sense them, and our anxieties feed off one another. As we become better at the skills of confrontation and speaking directly, the other person's anxiety is often calmed because we are more confident in the message we want to deliver and the outcome we want to have. They sense our good intent. They might know what they need to work on and feel some sense of relief the topic was discussed as they now feel they can approach us on it in a more productive way.

There are times, however, no matter how grounded we are, we feel ourselves becoming irritated or angry at issues or people around us. If they are pessimistic and depressed, we may start to feel a little down. If the other person is really up and then really down, we may start to experience a little bit of their roller coaster ride. In either of these examples, it just takes one person to call out what is happening, state their goal and need for help (if any), and move on. Anxiety is calmed by structure and clarity.

Emotions are a lot like weather. They come on quickly. They are variable and unpredictable. Self-awareness can help. Knowing what sets us off about other people gives us valuable information on how to respond versus react. Emotions can be unreliable when our beliefs are informed by inaccurate assumptions. Taking stock of how we are filtering information around us gives us even more data.

Gaining awareness of our blind spots shows us what is pulling our emotional strings. It enables us to become curious instead of giving in to being furious. Why do we allow people or situations to dictate our moods and decisions? What causes us to second-guess ourselves? How do we access and gain wisdom during chaotic times? How do we remain grounded and add value when everything appears to be a top priority?

Sometime today, we may be confronted by challenge or change. As a result, we may find ourselves in the grip of powerful negative emotions. Don't trust them. Rein them in. Test them. Reflect on them. Observe their initial power, and how focused attention dissipates their impact.

Our feelings, like the weather, will inevitably change. No one can maintain pure resentment, happiness, sadness, anger, or frustration forever. Pure emotion is the red flag we need to know that we no longer in neutral.

"You are responsible for
the energy you bring into a room."

— JILL BOLTE TAYLOR,
American neuroanatomist, author, and
inspirational public speaker

"Most folks are as happy as they
make up their minds to be."

— ABRAHAM LINCOLN,
American statesman and lawyer who served as the 16th
president of the United States

"I can be changed by what happens to me.
But I refuse to be reduced by it."

— MAYA ANGELOU,
American poet, singer, memoirist, and civil rights activist

"If your mind carries a heavy burden of past, you will
experience more of the same. The past perpetuates itself through lack of presence. The quality of your con-
sciousness at this moment is what shapes the future."

— ECKHART TOLLE,
German-Canadian author

Emotions are contagious. When we're in the presence of people who challenge us, we are more likely to take on some aspect of their emotional state. Anxiety, like the flu, likes to travel. However, if we are mentally prepared, we can create enough psychological distance to remain calm and neutral in the presence of volatility. Call out what is happening. Get curious about why the other person (or we) feel a certain way. State the goal (or request help), and move on.

The next time you encounter challenge or change working with others, be aware of your feelings. Catch yourself the next time you start to get upset, worried, frustrated, irritated or angry. Take a moment; do what you need to do to calm down and "unhook" yourself. Don't allow the other person's emotional state to become your emotional state.

Talk to a friend or trusted colleague about the ways you both can stay calm and neutral in the presence of an other's emotional static.

If you keep a journal for your own development, write down your thoughts about the power and the impact of positive and negative emotions.

The last time you were angry of frustrated, what happened to contribute to those feelings?

____

____

____

____

The last time you were enthusiastic and energized about your work, what happened to contribute to those feelings?

____

____

____

____

____

If you'd like to continue thinking about this idea in the future, check the box

At the end of the book, you can summarize all the practices that worked for you and start to generate your own curriculum.

There are situations and people that set me off. What can I learn about that?

Anger is one letter short of danger. When we are angry, we are reacting from our unconscious. We are not completely in control and unlikely to make the best choices.

The next time you are faced with a challenging person and tempted to lose your temper or give in to the temptation to react, take a moment to think about what you are doing.

"Anger: an acid that can do more harm
to the vessel in which it is stored than
to anything on which it is poured."

— SENECA,
Roman Stoic philosopher, statesman

It is a hard task to maintain emotional equilibrium when we have had our feelings hurt, careers sabotaged, plans disrupted, and our lives impacted by challenge and change. Sometimes an injustice has been committed and our anger is warranted. Deep wounds can leave a lasting memory that we carry around with us. And, when we can identify a person who hurt us, we have a focal point for our angst. Unless we can find the inner strength to forgive that person, we're likely to internalize our anger for years, even decades. Sometimes our pain can last a lifetime.

Anger turned inward results in depression, which impacts the health of our spirit and our bodies as well as our overall performance. Those are important enough reasons to learn how to create enough space for a considered response over giving in to immediate reactivity. Otherwise, we risk getting sucked up in a vortex of anger and turmoil.

To maintain openness is to maintain a certain sense of neutrality, where you can see both sides of a conflict, including your own, it's important to learn to see the situation from multiple angles. Don't let the "you or me" "us v them" tribalism swallow your civility. Don't succumb to the myth that being angry or indignant about an issue you care about is a sign of sophistication or complexity.

Awareness and perspective are key to attaining emotional equilibrium and it is our neutrality at times when everything around us is electric that gives us credibility.

Initial awareness is gained through reflection after an incident occurs. If we understand what the gap in our behavior is and know what it should be, we have a shot at catching ourselves in the act the next time. If we successfully catch ourselves in the moment, we get just enough time to make a different choice. When we catch ourselves enough times, we can spot a trigger coming rather than having it blindside us into rash reactivity. Seeing a trigger coming gives us even more time to choose a different reaction.

"I realized that if my thoughts immediately affect my body, I should be careful about what I think. Now if I get angry, I ask myself why I feel that way. If I can find the source of my anger, I can turn that negative energy into something positive."

— YOKO ONO,
Japanese-American multimedia artist, singer, songwriter and peace activist

"Anybody can become angry - that is easy, but to be angry with the right person and to the right degree and at the right time and for the right purpose, and in the right way - that is not within everybody's power and is not easy."

— ARISTOTLE,
Greek philosopher

"A man in a passion, rides a mad horse."

— BEN FRANKLIN,
American polymath, one of the Founding Fathers of the United States

"Anger is one letter short of danger."

— ELEANOR ROOSEVELT,
American political figure, diplomat and activist, former First Lady of the United States

 When furious, get curious. If you think you are about to lose your patience because you are some shade of angry (frustrated, irritated or annoyed)—take a beat, slow down and turn the attention onto yourself.

 Think about your own reactions to the situation and the decisions you are about to make. It is better to pause and reflect to determine a more thoughtful cause of action, or at minimum, think through alternatives.

 Talk to a friend or trusted colleague about the consequences of taking action when you are irritated, annoyed, frustrated, or angry. How do they impact others? How do they impact your own emotional health?

If you keep a journal for your own development, write
down your thoughts about the inevitable problems
that result from anger that is either expressed in inap-
propriate ways or held inside.

If you'd like to continue thinking about this idea in the
future, check the box

At the end of the book, you can summarize all the practices
that worked for you and start to generate your own curriculum.

2

I spend a lot of time trying to "play things out" in my head. There is preparing and there is spinning on situations that are not likely to happen. How can I better determine which is which?

Generally, there are two types of things to worry about: things within your control and things outside of your control. Once you distinguish between the two, spend your time on things within your control. Everything else will take care of itself.

"Worry is like a rocking chair:
it gives you something to do
but never gets you anywhere."

— ERMA BOMBECK,
American humorist, columnist and author

Go Beyond Worry

If we can think, we can worry. Even if we meditate every day, practice our faith, go to the gym after work, or practice yoga—we can also worry. Everyone with opposable thumbs and extra time on their hands gets bouts of discouragement and doubt, especially when we are engaged with challenge and change. We all find ourselves disrupted by people and situations out of our control.

So, where to take our worries? We can bring them to our practice. Bring them to church, to meditation, to yoga, and to the gym. Take them on a walk. Journal them. Worries are static that needs to be cleared from our bodies and our minds to make space for the creativity it takes to deal with a challenge. When we fail to clear that static, we tend to react because the only options we see are at the end of the behavior spectrum (fight or flight).

Ability for critical self-evaluation is critical for personal and professional development. By revisiting the events of the day, asking yourself basic questions like:

- What went well?

- Where did things start to go off the rails?

- What work remains unfinished?

There are many benefits to journaling, or even light note taking. First, we are creating written "data" of our progress. Over time, we can start to look back on our efforts and take note of our progression. Second, journaling helps with sleep as it helps us purge anxious thoughts or unfinished business that can cause our mind to spin up when it should be winding down. Journaling helps us lay to rest those last thoughts of the day, allowing it to close in reflection rather than avoidance. And last, it can give us a very literal understanding of something we may already intellectually know—that our first thoughts are never our fault.

The thoughts racing through our minds are part of our wiring and ways of coping. However, our judgments, impulses, will, and choice are all within our control. Just because these things are within your control does not mean they are not influenced by external factors: other people's opinions of you, physical sensations, etc. But ultimately, they are under your control because you can make a conscious choice to ignore your impulses or override the opinions of others.

There are things not in our control: how our body reacts, our property could get damaged or stolen, our reputation is in the hands of others, and anything that is not our own doing (basically all things external to our mind).

Consider an incident that you wish had played out differently and write about it. It can be anything from seeing someone at lunch, to a major meeting, to a person you actively avoided. Choose something that is not too emotionally jarring. List the aspects of it that were completely in your control and which were not. This might yield some initial insights on what is or is not in your control.

Here is an example:

> *Met with my boss today to discuss the latest customer escalation close rates. I was a little nervous going in since I'm not quite hitting my mark. We sat down and discussed what action steps I could take to get back on track by the end of the month. A lot of the suggestions were helpful.*

In My Control

- The intent to show up on time to the meeting

- Valuing my boss's opinion of me and my work

- The wish to reduce my close rates and turnaround times

- The desire to get actionable advice from my boss (if it'd help meet most of my goals)

- Conscious nervous thoughts/what I tell myself

Out Of My Control

- Actually showing up on time (another meeting might have run late)

- My boss's opinion of me

- Meeting my close targets (I can't force the engineering team to implement ALL my fixes!)

- Actually getting useful tips

- Automatic nervous thoughts and physical feelings of anxiety

The side of **In My Control** is filled more with results and the **Out Of My Control** side has more desires, wants, wishes, etc. Both the last points on both sides are automatic thoughts/sensations more or less—not everything in our bodies and minds are willed. We do not *choose* for our heart to race or hands to sweat, they just do. We do not *decide* to dwell in worst case scenarios, but our personalities might have compulsions to do so. However, once we notice these tendencies, we can choose (consciously) where to direct our thoughts, despite those automatic responses.

"People become attached to their burdens
sometimes more than the burdens are
attached to them."

— GEORGE BERNARD SHAW,
Irish playwright, critic, polemicist and political activist

"When I look back on all these worries, I remember
the story of the old man who said on his deathbed
that he had had a lot of trouble in his life,
most of which had never happened."

— WINSTON CHURCHILL,
British politician, army officer, and writer

"The reason why worry kills more people than work
is that more people worry than work."

— ROBERT FROST,
American poet

"If a problem is fixable,
if a situation is such that you can do something
about it, then there is no need to worry. If it's not
fixable, then there is no help in worrying.
There is no benefit in worrying whatsoever."

— THE DALAI LAMA,
Tibetan Buddhist

 We have worries. We also have solutions. Our challenge is to trust that we can solve a problem with creativity and considered response instead of reactivity.

 Divide your areas of concern into two categories: things within your control and things outside of your control. Focus on what is actually within your control. Do not waste time and energy worrying about anything else.

 Talk to a friend or trusted colleague about ways in which you can trust yourself more and worry less.

If you keep a journal for your own development, write down a few practical things you can do to overcome anxiety and worry.

____

____

____

____

____

____

____

____

____

____

If you'd like to continue thinking about this idea in the future, check the box

At the end of the book, you can summarize all the practices that worked for you and start to generate your own curriculum.

Empathy

Understanding our own emotions is only half of the work in a conversation. Learning how to constructively understand and respond to the emotions of others is also critical to our effectiveness at working with others: observe specific behaviors; be curious about the mood or emotion from another person; and, find a way to connect with them. Empathy helps develop our relationships.

- **Be compassionate.** When analyzing other people's motivation, know that you will never see the whole picture. Your task, on route to maturity, is to do your best to be kind, empathetic, and compassionate to people who challenge you.

- **Find patience.** We know the right path is to practice patience, especially when it's hard. Patience is a quality of emotional equilibrium and neutrality. Neutrality is where you enjoy the highest creativity, where you see the most alternatives to reactivity.

- **Learn from everyone, even them.** For whatever reason, there are people in our lives that we experience as difficult, don't respect, or that chafe us in some way. To remain effective in our work, these are the individuals who teach us humility, patience, empathy, and compassion.

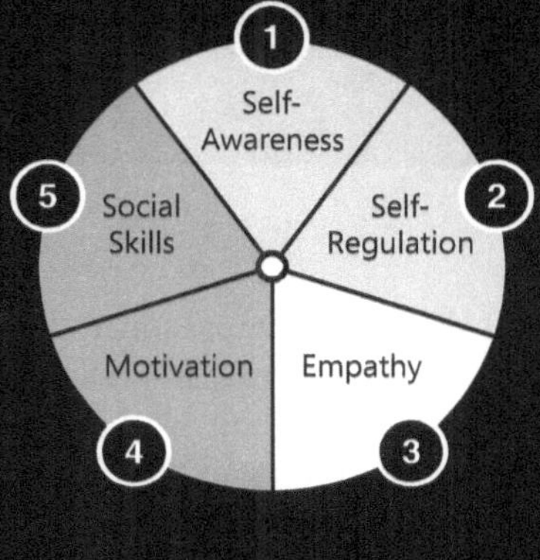

- **Check your filters.** Filters that cloud our ability to drive results with others have to do with how we interpret the: truth of the content we receive, quality of our relationship with the feedback giver, and impact of the feedback to our identities.

- **Ask more questions.** Asking questions is not just a way to bring another person along in an idea, it is a tool we can use to challenge our own thinking and slow us down. To explain a key concept means we know it inside and out and can synthesize and simplify that knowledge for others. Taking time to hear others into speech, to help them articulate what they are trying to say, as they are learning complex ideas requires patience and compassion for the learning process. While they are learning the idea, we are learning how to influence for positive impact.

3

I know I should be compassionate to everyone, not just the ones who are easy to get along with. It is hard to collaborate with people who always want something, who deal in transactions. I don't perceive them as motivated by a higher sense of mission. They ride my nerves, stretch my patience, and bring me to the edge. How do I get past that?

Yes, it's easy to say "be good to everyone" when the pressure isn't on. We are less judgmental of others when we have more reserves. It's hard, but not impossible, to treat everyone with respect—even those that ride our nerves.

"Could a greater miracle take place
than for us to look through each
other's eyes for an instant?
"

— HENRY DAVID THOREAU,
American essayist, poet, and philosopher

We have all heard of the Golden Rule, *treat others as we would want to be treated*. But when deadlines loom, management adds more priorities to our lists, and the stresses of home life get in the way—it is hard not to lash out. We perceive those around us as making our lives unnecessarily harder. Maybe we react emotionally or negatively. When someone seems to be litigating their way through challenging feedback, we are reminded to pause. Their reserves might be overdrawn. Our reserves might also be low. This is a time for compassion—why?

The mental processes of kindness, empathy, compassion need constant cultivation. When we are tired, discouraged, or overwhelmed, we don't always have the energy or the mental capacity to say something nice. Sometimes we don't have overwhelm to blame, we exist in toxic cultures where harassment is the norm. Respect, sometimes, just goes out the window. If being a high performer and if achieving personal and professional mastery is our ultimate goal, we need to hold ourselves to a higher standard than just "getting through the day."

Kindness, empathy, and compassion assume we have enough of those things for ourselves to give them to others. To give to others, we have to tend to ourselves, first. It sounds counterintuitive, almost selfish, or even wrong. However, when we have slept well, choose to eat good food, and surround ourselves with nourishing people, it is a lot easier to treat others well. It is easier, because we are taking care of ourselves.

Sometimes being kind to someone, particularly someone that is continually taking for themselves, is giving them a boundary. People who take, eventually hit a wall and learn that they need to find other ways of getting what they need.

Focusing on one thing to respect about someone who challenges us, taking time to forgive the small slights, and assuming the best intent from others pays dividends. For instance, we are not carrying around the tension, frustration, or anger of the impacts of their behavior. Instead, we are instead letting it roll off, or better yet—not impact our side of the tennis court. We are also modeling how we want to be treated. Our kindness, empathy or support might be the only small acts of kindness, empathy or support that person feels for their whole day. Imagine that for a second.

"Resentment is like drinking poison and waiting
for the other person to die."
— Carrie Fisher,
American actress, writer, and comedian

"Grudges are a waste of perfect happiness. Laugh.
Apologize. Let go of what you can't change."
— George Carlin,
American stand-up comedian, actor,
author, and social critic

"We think we listen, but very rarely do we listen with
real understanding, true empathy. Yet listening, of this
very special kind, is one of the most potent forces for
change that I know."
— Carl Rogers,
American psychologist

"Nobody cares how much you know, until
they know how much you care."
— Theodore Roosevelt,
American statesman, politician, conservationist, naturalist,
and writer; served as the 26th president of the United States

 When analyzing other people's motivation, know that you will never see the whole picture. Your task, on route to maturity, is to do your best to be kind, empathetic, and compassionate to people who challenge you.

 Think of a time when you judged someone's motivations too quickly. How did you feel then? How will you react in the future?

Reflect on your day. How do you think you were percieved by to the people you came in contact with?

 Talk to a friend or trusted colleague about the need to look for the best in others, even when it's a challenge.

If you keep a journal for your own development, write down your thoughts about practical ways you can apply the Golden Rule when you're dealing with people who challenge you, and you're under pressure to perform.

____

____

____

____

____

____

____

____

____

____

____

If you'd like to continue thinking about this idea in the future, check the box

At the end of the book, you can summarize all the practices that worked for you and start to generate your own curriculum.

 I'm having a hard time finding patience, especially when people are challenging. What advice do you have?

 We learn when we are young that patience is a virtue. Diplomacy shows us that patience is better than strength. These are both aspirational states for a reason—because they are hard when we are challenged by a person or situation. When we are tempted to get frustrated, we need to remember that patience pays us dividends and impatience buys on credit.

"Why is patience so important?
Because it makes us pay attention."

— Paulo Coelho,
Brazilian lyricist and novelist

It can be hard to be patient, compassionate and kind when we are trying to work through others during challenge and change. For example, when we perceive someone is under-performing, it's hard to be curious and understand why that may be happening—or that we might have anything to do with it. But we're human, and we fall short. We get easily irritated. We judge. We allow ourselves to get frustrated by others' shortcomings even though we show remarkable tolerance with our own.

It's much easier to spot under-performance in others than in ourselves. Whenever we point one finger toward someone else, there are four more pointing back at us. While the other might indeed be struggling, there are still things we can work on in ourselves.

What is patience? The dictionary tells us that Patience is "*the capacity to accept or tolerate delay, difficulty, or annoyance without getting angry or upset.*" We all have to contend with these circumstances throughout our days and lives. In doing so, we find our limits. We discover our tolerance.

We know we reach out limits when feelings like irritation, frustration, or anger show up like uninvited guests. These guests stay too long and they amplify what is already happening, making it a party you can't wait to leave. Here is where we realize that the more we don't want them to stay, the more they have no intention of leaving.

Instead of inviting anger to come in at all, we instead make a conscious effort to respond to "delay, difficult, and annoyance" in other ways. We can merely "tolerate" them, like bad guests they are. With practice, we can learn to accept them as a part of life—like in-laws, or those family members that tend to irritate us.

When we can do this—tolerate and accept delay, difficulty, or annoyance—something happens.

Patience is a form of compassion. We are not allowing ourselves to be spun up by the behavior of others—this helps us, first, then others. We are more present, capable of seeing the big picture, and likely to emotionally self-regulate. We are like a first-responder, calm at the scene, while others are spun up. Imagine if a first responder gave way to emotions of panic during a crisis, how ineffective they would be? How little value they would add?

We are less effective when we are impatient. When our systems are depleted, and stress is controlling our actions and reactions, our bodies and minds are not really our own.

Patience enables emotional equilibrium—the key to minimizing the extreme ride of life's ups and downs to the very high highs, and the very low lows. Emotional equilibrium keeps us in the middle, where satisfaction, contentment, meaning, and creative flow exist. When we are at the very top or bottom of life, we tend to only see very few options. In the middle, however, we see many more alternatives and solutions. The middle is where creativity exists.

When we see the correlation between patience and enhanced self-compassion and emotional equilibrium for ourselves, we can see the value in cultivating a daily practice.

"The two most powerful warriors are patience and time."
— LEO TOLSTOY,
Russian writer

"Water does not resist. Water flows. When you plunge your hand into it, all you feel is a caress. Water is not a solid wall, it will not stop you. But water always goes where it wants to go, and nothing in the end can stand against it. Water is patient. Dripping water wears away a stone. Remember you are half water. If you can't go through an obstacle, go around it. Water does."
— MARGARET ATWOOD,
American author, *The Penelopiad*

"Make your ego porous. Will is of little importance, complaining is nothing, fame is nothing. Openness, patience, receptivity, solitude is everything."
— RAINER MARIA RILKE,
Bohemian-Austrian poet and novelist

"It is very strange that the years teach us patience - that the shorter our time, the greater our capacity for waiting."
— ELIZABETH TAYLOR,
British-American actress, businesswoman, and humanitarian

 We know the right path is to practice patience, especially when it's hard. Patience is a quality of emotional equilibrium and neutrality. Neutrality is where you enjoy the highest creativity, where you see the most alternatives to reactivity.

 When you're dealing with challenge or change, it's easy to respond negatively and much, much harder to be patient—hard, but not impossible. Think about the ways patience pays dividends and impatience buys on credit.

 Talk to a friend or trusted colleague about the power of patience and how time plays a key role. Time can be the moment it takes to pause and reflect, or the years it takes to overcome difficulty.

If you keep a journal for your own development, write
down your thoughts about the rewards of patience
and the costs of impatience.

____

____

____

Think of a time when you were impatient.

____

How did it feel in your body?

____

What emotions did you feel?

____

What thoughts did you have?

____

When you reflect on it now how do you feel?

____

If you'd like to continue thinking about this idea in the
future, check the box

At the end of the book, you can summarize all the practices
that worked for you and start to generate your own curriculum.

There is a colleague who I don't get along with and would never work for—but they are a primary stakeholder of mine. How do I go along to get along?

We have all been told since we were children that there will be people with which we won't get along. And, in our jobs, we go a step further by focusing purely on the result, suggesting to ourselves, "we don't have to be best friends to get this done."

All team-working situations are fundamentally about working with other people. If you are open to receiving feedback, even from people you disagree with, then you will become, and be, a good person to work with in a team. It truly is as simple as that.

"All feedback is relevant, even if it's not true."

— FORD TAYLOR,
American author

One of the main skills blocking our ability to drive results with others is our feedback skills. So much attention has been focused on the giver, hoping the feedback lands well. Very little attention is paid to the receiver.

Giving and receiving feedback well is essential in any team-working situation. Being able to give clear and effective feedback to others is vital to keep the group process running effectively, and to plan. It also helps to ensure that we do not get irritated and angry with the way that others are behaving. It follows that we also need to be able to receive feedback gracefully, and then act on it calmly—regardless of what we may think of the other person.

Hearing comments from people we don't respect, don't like, and can't stand to be around is especially important. Because of our desire to avoid them, they likely become even more critical to our success. We can also learn the most from them. Funny how that works, isn't it?

As challenging as it may be for us, we have to find ways to work well with a broad spectrum of people to build good and productive working and other relationships. To drive results with others *we need to see the relationship as at least as important as the task in hand.*

Read that again: *we need to see the relationship as at least as important as the task in hand.* That is a value statement, stating: people are as important as results.

Most people pay lip service to the idea. It is only when we are confronted with pressure or challenged by another person's performance that we must confront our beliefs about how we value results, and people.

How can we collaborate, share plans and ideas, and work together to build a better whole? How can we promote a cooperative climate where everyone is invited to contribute?

By actively, intentionally managing our relationships. We may not profit from some of our closest connections, but the bad ones will result in heavy losses. In this way, *everyone* is our teacher—especially the people we can't seem to get along with.

We need to actively seek out opportunities for deeper connection. We do this by first questioning our thoughts and feelings about how we feel around them. What is it about the other person that sets us off? Do they shut us down, interrupt, ignore our contributions, get aggressive when others disagree with them, bully us into agreement, frustrate us with their lack of knowledge, slow pace of thinking, or shallow opinions?

Our experience is our experience *and it is valid.* And, we need to become curious about what data we are selecting, and how that data informs our assumptions and beliefs. We emotionally react and take action on those perceptions.

How we perceive others can be felt. On some level, conscious or unconscious, they know what we are thinking.

But if we slow ourselves down, we are in learning mode about our thoughts and feelings. We ask more questions than we have judgments, helping us develop a stronger understanding of the people around us. From there, we are more likely to make better decisions.

"I cannot make the universe obey me.
I cannot make other people conform to my
own whims and fancies. I cannot make
even my own body obey me."

— THOMAS MERTON,
American Trappist monk, writer, theologian,
and social activist

"When another person makes you suffer, it is because
he suffers deeply within himself, and his suffering is
spilling over. He does not need to be punished; He
needs help. That's the message he is sending."

— THICH NHAT HANH,
Vietnamese Buddhist monk and peace activist

"In the practice of tolerance, one's enemy
is the best teacher."

— DALI LAMA,
Tibetan Bhuddist

"If it was necessary to tolerate in other people
everything that one permits oneself,
life would be unbearable."

— GEORGES COURTELINE,
French dramatist and novelist

 For whatever reason, there are people in our lives that we experience as difficult, don't respect, or that chafe us in some way. To remain effective in our work, these are the individuals who teach us humility, patience, empathy, and compassion.

 When you're dealing with a particular person who presents a challenge to you, it's easy to judge them as less than—less knowledgeable, less competitive, less… anything. Think about what they have to offer, why they are in the role they are in, and what you can learn from them.

 Talk to a friend or trusted colleague about people you have unexpectedly learned something valuable. Consider if you could have learned that lesson from someone more agreeable.

If you keep a journal for your own development, write down your thoughts about the opportunities and missed opportunities of viewing everyone, even people you wouldn't initially suspect, to be your teacher.

____

____

____

____

____

____

____

____

____

____

If you'd like to continue thinking about this idea in the future, check the box

At the end of the book, you can summarize all the practices that worked for you and start to generate your own curriculum.

There are a few people I work with whom I just can't accept their feedback. When they talk, even if it's valuable, I have a hard time hearing it *from them*.

We all have hidden (and sometimes not-so-hidden) biases that interfere with our ability to listen and empathize. Common biases center around visible factors such as age, race, and gender. But communication goes much, much deeper than that.

Filters that cloud our ability to drive results with others have everything to do with how accurate we determine the content to be, how we relate to the person giving us the feedback, or if the feedback threatens our sense of identity. In short, check yourself before you wreck yourself.

"Sinners often speak the truth.
And saints have led people astray.
Examine what is said,
not the one who says it."

— Anthony de Mello,
Indian Jesuit priest and psychotherapist

There is no shortage of feedback coming to us—from bosses, colleagues, friends, family—but it does little to shift certain patterns. Most attention is given to the feedback giver; when we have comments for someone else, we want to "do it right" so the comments "land." When we are on the receiving end, we decide whether to make use of the feedback and improve—or we decide to ignore it.

When someone gives us feedback, our first reaction is to check for accuracy. If we are feeling defensive, we might want to litigate every aspect of it in an attempt to diminish its impact.

Three common triggers cause feedback to go awry: truth, relationship, and identity. Truth Triggers are the content of the feedback. We get triggered when we feel the *content* of the feedback is off base. Relationship triggers come from the *particular person* who is giving the feedback. If we believe the person has no credibility or has treated us with little respect, then this affects how we respond to the feedback. Identity Triggers threaten who I AM, making us question our identity and the story we tell ourselves about who we are.

A strategy we can use when we feel the content of feedback is off base include separating appreciation (expressions of gratitude), coaching (expressions designed to accelerate our learning) and evaluation (expressions designed to rank, assess, or rate us). For example, imagine if you had just finished a painting and showed it to a friend who is an artist. If she told you twelve things to fix and you were hoping for, "Nice job. Keep working on it," you'd be upset. Alternatively, if you wanted critical comments to improve your work, you would be disappointed if she just said, "Nice job. Keep working on it." Know what kind of feedback you are getting.

A suggestion for handling feedback even when the relationship with the feedback giver is challenging is to untangle the what from the who. If we feel someone has treated us poorly, it is difficult to separate the feedback from the relationship. When you respond to feedback with, "Who are you to say that?" these are really two different issues – the content of the feedback and how the giver speaks to us. It is best to have two different conversations about these two different topics.

To get the most out of feedback when it threatens your identity, you must understand how your coping mechanisms lay and temperament affect your story. What causes one person shame might not even register with someone else. Understanding our own temperaments and how we are wired can help us deal with triggers that hit our core sense of identity.

"True intuitive expertise is learned from prolonged experience with good feedback on mistakes."
— DANIEL KAHNEMAN,
Israeli-American psychologist and economist

"The single biggest problem in communication is the illusion that it has taken place."
— GEORGE BERNARD SHAW,
Irish playwright, critic, polemicist and political activist

"If your actions inspire others to dream more, learn more, do more and become more, you are a leader."
— JOHN QUINCY ADAMS,
American statesman, diplomat, lawyer, and diarist;
6th US President

"All that is valuable in human society depends upon the opportunity for development accorded the individual."
— ALBERT EINSTEIN,
German-born theoretical physicist

 Filters that cloud our ability to drive results with others have to do with how we interpret the: truth of the content we receive, quality of our relationship with the feedback giver, and impact of the feedback to our identities.

 When we think that our traits and abilities are "fixed," we believe we aren't going to change. Those with a "growth" identity believe they are ever evolving and growing, so any piece of feedback is actually welcome because it helps them improve.

Each exercise in this pocket guide is an opportunity for you to practice and explore working with and through others, exploring topics from their perspective. Use the prompts to explore your reactions around content, relationships, and identity when hearing the other person's point of view. How much can you really hear?

 Talk to a friend or trusted colleague about your experiences receiving feedback. Consider if you could have leaned into the content a bit more if the relationship hadn't gotten in the way.

If you keep a journal for your own development, write down your thoughts about the feedback you have received from particular people, making it hard to understand their message. Now that you have had some distance, what can you learn about yourself from the experience?

____

____

____

____

____

____

____

____

____

____

If you'd like to continue thinking about this idea in the future, check the box

At the end of the book, you can summarize all the practices that worked for you and start to generate your own curriculum.

3

When I feel strongly about a particular solution to a problem, I'm usually right. Sometimes it frustrates me to have to listen to others, though I make time for it. Sometimes I just want to hush the other voices in the room so I can get on to other things. How do I manage this urge?

Being right, often, can be both a blessing and a curse. On the one hand, people can take your recommendations to the bank because they are solid. On the other, the best solutions generally come from a diverse set of thinking and being open to a third solution (your ideas + others = ??) invites creativity. This is a good time for asking questions—but be strategic.

"It is better to debate a question without settling it than to settling a question without debating it."

— JOSEPH JOUBERT,
French moralist and essayist

Questions have the power to change lives by forcing us to reckon with a core truth or make a difficult decision. Challenging a team to think differently can jump start creative problem solving and unlock log jams from the status quo. Asking the right question, at the right time, with just the right people can make-or-break organizations, helping them reframe entire industries.

Questions are all well and good, but leaders must be decisive. They must have the courage to see and say what others fear. They stand in the center of the fire, sitting with the discomfort of making hard decisions. They have to live with the power that comes from both failure and success. From this perspective, leaders have a more complete view, more information. They have strong judgment and good instincts. Leaders that view management, leadership and driving results with others as an ongoing discipline, seek diverse perspectives and work to disconfirm their own beliefs in the presence of the right information.

But, if we are right *just enough*, we can get stale, lazy, insular and complacent. Being right all the time can create a team dependency where others stop thinking about things we know about and stop challenging us with new ideas, rendering us out of touch. Being right all the time can contribute to group think, where we make decisions in a way that discourages creativity or individual responsibility.

Managing our reactivity to others' input—as a waste of time, ill-informed, or taking too much time, etc.—develops us as much as it empowers them. It forces us to develop patience. Patience can help us think more comprehensively.

What if they don't know what they don't know? Beyond listening to repeat what the other person said, we are attempting to hear the other into speech. That is, we are listening to hear what they are trying to say, but cannot fully express. We listen, adding subtext that isn't expressed, or context from the bigger picture to help extend their idea. How can curiosity help us challenge or confirm our assumptions about others' knowledge?

What if they should know more but do not? It is up to us to suspend judgment and create space for curiosity. What knowledge do they have that we do not that would be beneficial in cultivating a new perspective?

The ability to understand others' poorly expressed or incomplete thoughts and concerns as well as their underlying meanings helps develop their thinking (and ours) and increases our influence and mentoring skills. Developing others at times when we can dominate requires us to be patient, recognize different values and styles, and value others' unique characteristics or strengths.

In addition to bringing our knowledge and expertise to a conversation, bringing three or four thoughtful, even provocative questions to every conversation helps advance the thinking in the room, *advancing a conversation adds value.*

"A wise man can learn more from a foolish question than a fool can learn from a wise answer."
— BRUCE LEE,
Hong Kong-American actor, director, martial artist, martial arts instructor, and philosopher

"I think that probably the most important thing about our education was that it taught us to question even those things we thought we knew."
— THABO MBEKI,
South African politician and second president of South Africa

"Fear is a question. What are you afraid of and why? Our fears are a treasure house of self-knowledge if we explore them"
— MARILYN FRENCH,
Radical feminist American author

"He must be very ignorant for he answers every question he is asked."
— VOLTAIRE,
French Enlightenment writer, historian, and philosopher

 Being right, often, can be both a blessing and a curse. Be strategic with your contributions. Balance them by asking clarifying questions. Our hastiness to be right or to dominate comes at a cost. We miss an opportunity to develop others, as well as ourselves.

 Asking questions is not just a way to bring another person along in an idea, it is a tool we can use to challenge our own thinking and slow us down. To explain a key concept means we know it inside and out and can synthesize and simplify that knowledge for others. Taking time to hear others into speech as they are learning complex ideas requires patience and compassion for the learning process. While they are learning the idea, we are learning how to influence for positive impact.

 Talk to a friend or trusted colleague about the times when you've worked with a colleague, mentor or boss that had a gift for hearing people into speech or making the complex easier to understand. What qualities did they possess that helped them communicate and influence with impact?

If you keep a journal for your own development, write down your thoughts about a time when you needed to slow down in order to influence a colleague.

____

____

____

____

____

Did it feel like you had to "wait" for them to catch up? Did you enjoy the process of slowing down in order to go fast again? How did it feel to you to influence another?

____

____

____

____

____

If you'd like to continue thinking about this idea in the future, check the box

At the end of the book, you can summarize all the practices that worked for you and start to generate your own curriculum.

4

Understand Motivation

There is no direct line to happiness from external definitions of success, like money, titles, rank, and material rewards. Having a sense of mission, passion, or fascination with what we do leads to sustained attachment and motivation with our work. Strong motivation increases clarity of decision making and priorities.

- **Develop a practice.** We make decisions more than anything else. Filtering information effectively forces us to learn crucial skills of prioritization and delegation—skills that enable or block our advancement. When the stakes are high and the pressure is on, learning how to embrace a daily practice increases our chances of not only survival but effective performance. Learning how to prioritize and delegate information for ourselves, first, helps us drive results more effectively with others.

- **Focus on the small.** The word "iterate" is now overused jargon, but it is effective in pushing our learning, leadership and overall development forward. Focusing on the small wins helps combat the all or nothing mentality that creeps in when we are overwhelmed, looking for direction, and determining what reasonable next steps should be.

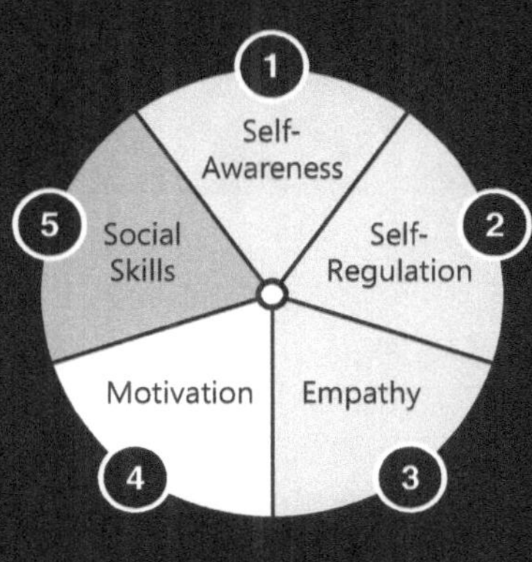

- **Hold tension.** Motivation is not a constant thing that is always there for us. As it comes and goes, managing the in-between time feels insurmountable because we think the goal is to maintain a constant state of high motivation. In fact, the goal is to maintain the in-between space more effectively. Managing our feelings helps us maintain an emotional equilibrium giving us greater connection to the feel of our work.

- **Find stamina.** When a new context pops up it teases the brain into thinking it's a new set of circumstances which can allow for a new set of strategies, but that is the very moment we need to be just as intentional about our practice. Success is not a goal, but a byproduct of consistent effort.

- **Feed the seeds, not the weeds.** Like a seed, we are equipped with everything we need to succeed. Contributions to upward spirals yield seeds; contributions to downward spirals yields weeds. We don't require perfect conditions. In fact, persistence amidst challenge and change is what serves as the catalyst for growth.

I know the big picture of what needs to get done. Yet, I'm overwhelmed by the sheer volume of information coming my way. The email, meetings, ad hoc requests, random problems on the team—add travel to the mix—and it makes focusing on a single thing very hard.

It's a cliché to say that today's employees are deluged with data. We know that sometimes we can get lost in the tactics and forget the strategy we are trying to execute. Developing effective daily practices are key to survival.

"Adventure is just bad planning."

— ROALD AMUNDSEN,
Norwegian explorer,
led the first expedition to traverse
the Northwest Passage by sea

1. Review your overarching strategy.

2. Review daily goals as they align to that strategy, reflect on where most of your energy will be needed and where you can have the most strategic impact.

3. Block your schedule and use reminders

4. Tally incomplete tasks and carry the balance to the next day.

5. Reflect on the day. What went well? What did you learn? How present and strategic were you? What impact did you have?

6. Repeat.

Most of us skip the first step. We attend the same kickoff as everyone else, but we are thinking about what needs to get done, not *why* we are doing it. Answering "what's it all for?" at the start of the day is a good reminder and grounding activity that can help motivate and help us catch a view of the forest before we descend into the trees. Learning how to prioritize and delegate information for ourselves, first, helps us drive results more effectively with others

Reading through it, a daily checklist might sound tedious and uninspiring. Keeping notebooks, calendar blocking, setting reminders, and taking time at the start and end of the day are all very important habits to maintaining progress—but they aren't the stuff of heroic stories. Nor do they give us the same bump of satisfaction that completing an ad-hoc request for a high-level manager or stepping in to save a drowning project.

Filtering the minutia of the day forces us to learn crucial skills of prioritization and delegation—skills required at every level of our advancement. We learn to separate the urgent from the important. Miscalculations can have unintended consequences as well as positive impact, regardless if we directly manage a team. If 100 requests or opportunities come to us, not all will align with our goals. There will be some percentage we will have to ignore or delegate to other stakeholders. We can only absorb so much.

Reaching greatness, however we define it for ourselves, requires focus on consistent and long-term personal performance. In the book *Great by Choice*, author Jim Collins set out to answer this question: *Why do some companies thrive in uncertainty, even chaos, and others do not?* He finds the answer in the story of two explorers, Amundsen and Scott, who led separate teams on an expedition race to the South Pole in 1911. The journey there and back was roughly 1,400 miles, which is equivalent to a round-trip from New York City to Chicago.

While both teams would be traveling the same distance as each other through extremely harsh weather conditions, each team took an entirely different approach to the journey. Scott's team would walk as far as possible on the good weather days and then rest up on the bad days to conserve energy.

Conversely, Amundsen's team adhered to a strict regimen of consistent progress by walking 20 miles every day no matter what the weather. While on good days Amundsen's team was very capable of walking further, Amundsen was adamant that they walk no more than 20 miles each day to conserve their energy.

Which one succeeded? The team that took consistent action.

Instead of constantly changing course, making aggressive moves, and taking big risks, Amundsen came up with a plan, and carefully, methodically, and consistently stuck with that plan. His team moved ever towards their long-term goals instead of getting sidetracked by short-term temptations, fears, and changing circumstances—and arrived on time. They didn't panic during stormy periods, nor did they expand too aggressively during good times. Scott's team that only traveled on good days ended up dying on the journey.

When the stakes are high and the pressure is on, learning how to embrace a daily practice increases our chances of not only survival but effective performance.

Applying this idea to your own day to day, a morning routine can begin as simply as asking:

…what do I want to think?

…what do I want to feel?

…what do I want to do?

Wrapping things up at the end of the day, reflect on the day's learning, be specific:

…what did I learn today?

…what new thing did I try I try today?

…what risk did I take?

…did I remain in integrity with my Craft?

…how can I improve?

…how can I amplify my knowledge and share what I know?

Consider these questions, or develop your own, but determine what 20 miles looks like for you, and stick to it.

"I may say that this is the greatest factor: the way in which the expedition is equipped, the way in which every difficulty is foreseen, and precautions taken for meeting or avoiding it. Victory awaits him who has everything in order, luck, people call it. Defeat is certain for him who has neglected to take the necessary precautions in time, this is called bad luck."

— ROALD AMUNDSEN,
Norwegian explorer, led the first expedition to
traverse the Northwest Passage by sea

"In no department can a leader spend time more profitably than in the selection of the men who are to accomplish the work."

— DOUGLAS MAWSON,
Australian geologist, Antarctic explorer, and academic

"The time to prepare for your next expedition is when you have just returned from a successful trip."

— ROBERT PEARY,
American explorer and United States Navy officer

We make decisions more than anything else. Filtering information effectively forces us to learn crucial skills of prioritization and delegation—skills that enable or block our advancement. When the stakes are high and the pressure is on, learning how to embrace a daily practice increases our chances of not only survival but effective performance. Learning how to prioritize and delegate information for ourselves, first, helps us drive results more effectively with others.

Commit to a daily practice. Determine what activities you will embrace to develop a more disciplined approach to managing your day. Pay attention to your level of task absorption in a given day and its emotional impact.

Talk to a friend or trusted colleague about the times you've been successful in a specific practice. Maybe you were trying to get better at time management and blocked off your mornings. Maybe it was reading a book a week. What were you trying to learn, and what practice did you adopt? What kept you motivated?

If you keep a journal for your own development, write down what practices you use to manage yourself.

____

____

____

____

How are they effective? Ineffective?

____

____

____

____

How can they be improved?

____

____

____

____

If you'd like to continue thinking about this idea in the future, check the box ☐

At the end of the book, you can summarize all the practices that worked for you and start to generate your own curriculum.

When I'm stuck or overwhelmed, everything feels important. It's like I've lost my ability to prioritize or even filter information. Where do I start?

You start where you are, plus one step.

When our stress exceeds our ability to cope, feelings of anger, fear, anxiety or guilt can be more pronounced.

Why? because we are releasing higher amounts of the "stress hormone" cortisol, leaving us overloaded with intense anxiety. At the same time, our serotonin stores, the chemical that helps our bodies fight off depression and anxiety, start to deplete. This combination causes the intense feeling of total despair associated with being overwhelmed.

"Small wins are a steady application
of a small advantage."

— CHARLES DUHIGG,
American journalist and non-fiction author

Whenever we are in a slump, it is often because we have too much going on in our lives or pressure as increased beyond our standard way of coping. Pressure can make even the smallest to-do list seem untenable, sapping our energy and motivation.

One of the most common mistakes goal-oriented people make is that they try to accomplish too many goals at once. We cannot maintain energy and focus (the two most important things in accomplishing a goal) if we are trying to do two or more goals at once. For example, most people fail at losing weight because they try to go to the gym and adjust their diet, and change their sleep patterns.

Choosing one goal, for now, and focusing on it completely, might sound hard. We can always do our other goals when we have accomplished our One Goal.

If we are having a hard time getting started, it may be because our goals are not reasonable. If we want to get in shape, for example, we may be thinking that we must do intense workouts 5 days a week. That is an appropriate goal for someone already in shape. To get in shape, we need to take smaller actions. The problem is, we do not respect the result that comes from a daily walk, or 2 workouts a week. But it works. We may want to do more, but just sticking to our initial commitment helps mitigate failure, relapse, and regression to old habits.

Everyone understands the think-small approach when it applies to personal goals. It makes sense to practice on small climbs before tackling Mt. Everest. But how does this work when we switch the context to the workplace?

Small bets. The myth of progress and innovation is that it comes from bold solutions requiring outsized risk. Sometimes, that is true. We go all in, bet the farm, and when it doesn't pan out, we're sunk. On the other hand, what if we never take the gamble? Fearful of what we might lose, we sit on our hands and embrace the status quo.

Whether we are talking about personal goals, workplace innovation, or our own learning process, we can make significant change taking reasoned actions. We need to experiment more—not with our health, or work prototypes, but *ourselves* (our learning, our leadership, and our overall development). Some of the most creative talents in the world—from Steve Jobs to Frank Gehry, made small bets to learn and grow. They didn't bet it all, all the time.

Small bets provide quick answers. What small bets can you make about:

- how to prioritize our time?

- who to delegate to on our team?

- what direction to take our strategy?

- increasing our network of influence?

- how to evolve the mission of our organization?

- what our succession plan should be?

"We don't have to engage in grand, heroic actions to participate in the process of change. Small acts, when multiplied by millions of people, can transform the world."

— HOWARD ZINN,
American historian, playwright, and socialist thinker

"A small win is a concrete, complete, implemented
outcome of moderate importance. By itself,
one small win may seem unimportant.
A series of wins at small but significant tasks,
however, reveals a pattern that may attract allies,
deter opponents, and lower resistance to
subsequent proposals. Small wins are
controllable opportunities that produce
visible results."

— KARL E. WEICK,
American organizational theorist

"You can get a great deal done from almost any position in an organization if you focus on small wins and you don't mind others getting the credit."

— ROGER SAILLANT,
Executive Director of The Fowler Center for Business

The word "iterate" is one of the most overused bits of jargon, but it is effective in pushing our learning, leadership and overall development forward. Focusing on the small wins helps combat the all or nothing mentality that creeps in when we are overwhelmed, looking for direction, and determining what reasonable next steps should be.

When we are in need of direction, focusing on the small is what helps us shape appropriate goals. Appropriate challenges are what move us forward.

Talk to a friend or trusted colleague about the times when you've felt overwhelmed or unsure of how to make progress. Have you ever bitten off too much? What helped you move forward?

If you keep a journal for your own development, write down your feelings and reactions to setting small goals.

____

____

____

____

____

Looking at what came up for you, what constructive insights can you gain about the next steps you need to take?

____

____

____

____

____

If you'd like to continue thinking about this idea in the future, check the box

At the end of the book, you can summarize all the practices that worked for you and start to generate your own curriculum.

I got a major win and feel great! or, Things could not be worse.

There are times when the wind is at our back. Our manager is pleased, our teams are humming, the market is relatively quiet. We had a good day. We are optimistic; we take a vacation.

There are times when the headwinds are so strong, if we let go of the rope, we'll fall off the boat. Our manager has a communication style that challenges us, and it feels like we can't do anything right. Our team feels fragmented, and the market questions our ethics or performance. Today was terrible. There is no way we are taking a vacation.

"Inspiration exists, but it has
to find you working."

— Pablo Picasso,
Spanish painter, sculptor, ceramicist,
poet and playwright

It can be hard to stay on the roller coaster when the highs are really high, and the lows are really low. These are precisely the times when the idea of emotional equilibrium sounds even more theoretical and out of touch than ever—and, when they are needed the most. We might be advocating for a particular solution or hoping for a certain outcome. We feel desperate to drive our agenda—or else. Or, things might be going well, making us even more likely to discount the idea. When overwhelm strikes—and it strikes us all—and we find ourselves so far in the hole we can no longer see out, the idea of 'emotional equilibrium' doesn't even make sense.

Motivation is not a constant thing that is always there for us. It ebbs and flows, like the tide. It never leaves permanently. It will always come back.

Managing the slump between enjoying the headwind of progress and suffering the tailwind struggle can last minutes, hours, or years. We cannot maintain life wholly at one end of that spectrum.

Emotional equilibrium, neutral space, is our goal. When we have both headwind and tailwind in sight we can better manage our movement toward one and away from the other as needed. Why would we ever move toward tailwind? How else would we grow and develop?

Managing our feelings helps us see beyond our immediate experience. If we are in a state of feeling overwhelmed, our emotions are generally running higher than normal. When strong emotions take over, our brain produces an influx of physiological sensations, an increase of the stress hormones adrenaline and cortisol, often resulting in difficulty accessing our resources for calming down and executive functioning. In the most simple terms, we aren't seeing reality clearly.

If we succumb to our feelings about anything (a person, a situation, a discussion, etc.) the "data" we gather is by nature incomplete since we are mentally incapable (at that moment) of taking a broader view.

This kind of overwhelm can occur from anything like the frustration we experience when we learn something new, to adding that "last brick" to our load when we take on too much (no matter how much of an expert we are).

When we maintain an emotional equilibrium we have the ability to more adeptly switch between the big picture and the focus it takes to get our jobs done. We also have a greater connection to the feel of our work. We are able to muster more enthusiasm, get 'into the groove' or 'find flow' with greater ease. Time slows down, and we can see more alternatives than we could if we were to just react. Emotions that come up as we deal with the struggle of regaining our competency again—frustration, anxiety, sadness, anger, boredom—can be painful, and they create static as we connect to our work. To maintain a more neutral state we need to focus on the small wins, learn to ask for help, and develop a practice until your motivation returns again.

"Your emotions are the slaves to your thoughts,
and you are the slave to your emotions."

— ELIZABETH GILBERT,
American author

"One ought to hold on to one's heart;
for if one lets it go, one soon
loses control of the head too."

— FRIEDRICH NIETZSCHE,
German philosopher

"In order to move on, you must understand
why you felt what you did and why you
no longer need to feel it."

— MITCH ALBOM,
American author, journalist, dramatist, and musician

"If you do not have control over your mouth,
you will not have control over your future."

— GERMANY KENT,
American print and broadcast journalist

 Motivation is not a constant thing that is always there for us. As it comes and goes, managing the in-between time feels insurmountable because we think the goal is to maintain a constant state of high motivation. In fact, the goal is to maintain the in between space more effectively.

 Managing our *feelings* helps us maintain an emotional equilibrium giving us greater connection to the *feel* of our work. Take time to reflect on highs and lows on your team or in your organization. Consider the connection (and fluency) you felt to your work during those times.

 Talk to a friend or trusted colleague about the times when you've felt headwind and tailwind in your career. How did you slide between the two states?

If you keep a journal for your own development, write down a time when feelings kept you from connecting to the feel of your work. (e.g., anxiety managing others for the first time; frustration when not achieving a professional goal, etc.)

____

____

____

What makes you most effective as you head toward progress?

____

____

____

What tactics helped you most as you worked out of tailwind?

____

____

____

If you'd like to continue thinking about this idea in the future, check the box

At the end of the book, you can summarize all the practices that worked for you and start to generate your own curriculum.

4

I've achieved a lot this year. I corrected some missteps and successfully increased my scope. Sometimes I feel like I'm out of strength. I'm just tapped. What can I do?

When you need strength, turn inward. Take time to breathe, reflect, and prioritize your energies. Don't try to do everything at once, or please everyone around you—that is the impossible.

"You mature as far as your understanding
of what it's going to take, and you
increase your stamina. You don't let
frustration overtake you when
you're looking for change."

— EDDIE VEDDER,
American musician, multi-instrumentalist
and singer-songwriter

Understanding our own motivations help us understand our decisions with greater clarity. Setting a goal, focusing on making progress, and holding tension of tipping forward are skills required for achievement. We can see this in personal goals like losing weight or quitting smoking. The same holds true for professional goals like earning promotions or dealing with significant increases in responsibility. The problem is, we know what the challenge of setting goals and achieving them looks like. We're less familiar with the challenge of maintenance. Because of that we set ourselves up for "loops of pain" where we achieve only to lose, over and over again.

Maintaining and sustaining that progress require a different kind of diligence and stamina. Before, we had goals we felt were almost out of reach. They forced us to stretch. After we achieve those results, we plateau for a bit as we negotiate life in our smaller bodies, healthier circle of friends, or enjoy the hum of our high performing teams.

After a while we forget how hard it was to achieve. We slack off a bit here and there. We stop going to the gym as often. We sneak a cigarette here and there. We stop engaging in the many strategies that helped us enable and empower our teams. Before we know it, we've gained some of the weight back, find ourselves wrestling with more frequent nicotine attacks, and feel overwhelmed by team dynamics in a way we weren't just two months ago—when we were still working *toward* our goals.

When did the shift occur? What did we tell ourselves in those moments? How did we let ourselves off the hook?

"I can skip the gym. It's just this week." *Can we?* "I can sneak a cigarette. It's only at lunch." *Should we?* "I have a demo due next week, and several days of workshops. I don't need to be as diligent about managing my day as I am when I have back to back meetings. I can manage it in my head. I don't need to check in with the team as much. They have it covered." *Really? Do they?*

Not always. If it took going to the gym every day to lose weight, quitting cold turkey to quit smoking, and employing certain strategies for a well-performing team to achieve its goals (like clear goals, frequent communication, follow through, etc.)—we likely need to persist with them in order to remain successful.

The behaviors we permit to slip enable us to slack off. Those are the red flags we need to pay attention to. When a new context pops up it teases the brain into thinking it is a new set of circumstances, but that is the moment we need to be just as intentional about our practice. When our routine gets disrupted—a VP has an ad hoc request, a big meeting date gets moved up, a day long workshop pops up on our calendars—we think we can relax our grip on the strategies that earned our success. That is why holidays make it hard to maintain weight goals. Holidays are an obvious disruption to our routine. Success is not a goal, but a byproduct of an intentional practice and consistent effort.

"Anyone whose goal is 'something higher' must expect someday to suffer vertigo. What is vertigo? Fear of falling? No, Vertigo is something other than fear of falling. It is the voice of the emptiness below us which tempts and lures us, it is the desire to fall, against which, terrified, we defend ourselves."

— MILAN KUNDERA,
Czech-born French writer

"We are what we repeatedly do. Excellence, then, is not an act but a habit."

— WILL DURANT,
American writer, historian, and philosopher

"That's been one of my mantras – focus and simplicity. Simple can be harder than complex: You have to work hard to get your thinking clean to make it simple. But it's worth it in the end because once you get there, you can move mountains."

— STEVE JOBS,
American business magnate, entrepreneur,
industrial designer, investor,
and media proprietor

 When a new context pops up it teases the brain into thinking it's a new set of circumstances which can allow for a new set of strategies, but that is the very moment we need to be just as intentional about our practice. Success is not a goal, but a byproduct of consistent effort.

 Think about times when you slipped on a goal that took a lot of effort to achieve. Now think of what you told yourself you did or did not need to do. What could you have done differently?

 Talk to a friend or trusted colleague about the many red flags we get and ignore when it comes to maintaining a hard-earned goal. What do they look like? Do they have anything in common?

If you keep a journal for your own development, write down your thoughts about maintaining and sustaining goals.

____

____

____

____

What was your goal, and what did it feel like to initially achieve your goal?

____

____

____

When did you start to slack off on that goal, and why? What did you tell yourself?

____

____

____

If you'd like to continue thinking about this idea in the future, check the box

At the end of the book, you can summarize all the practices that worked for you and start to generate your own curriculum.

I recovered well from some negative feedback and can accomplish a come-back pretty well. But there are "tipping points" where I find I'm right back where I started. How can I manage that more effectively?

Maintaining and sustaining progress can be harder than achieving the initial goal. Sometimes we get bored because the challenge is different—it's not as in-your-face. Other times, we take it for granted—as if that accomplishment was always ours and forever will be. The truth is, unless what we sought just comes naturally (and it likely does not) we need to re-earn that accomplishment every day.

"Complaining is one of the ego's favorite strategies for strengthening itself."

— ECKHART TOLLE,
German-Canadian author

Much like managing the neutral middle between highs and lows of the day to day, is the importance of maintaining the very visible progress of turning around a team or an organization, from low functioning to high functioning. The key is having a clear vision for the outcome and cultivating in that direction. First, distinguish the weeds from the seeds.

Pull The Weeds

Like gardens, our minds, teams and organizations need constant tending. Negative thinking is a lot like a noxious vine, allowed to destroy and crowd out positivity. They can easily make us feel "out of control." Try this mind game when you need to weed out the negativity and regain peace of mind. Give it a go for your current reflection and come back to it as a potential strategy when you need it again.

- Set a timer for 1 minute. Write down as many negative thoughts as you can, even if they sound crazy.

Negative thinking, like weeds, needs to be constantly managed. Optimism needs to be planted and nurtured. If we don't do these things *for ourselves*, we are ill-prepared for the arduous tasks that lay ahead. Our work then truly does become exhausting. These sentiments aren't a promise for a primrose path. They are the guidelines for perseverance.

Plant Seeds

Be still. Listen to your thoughts come, and go, like dandelion seeds in the breeze. If you are thinking something negative, watch that thought intensify and fade out again as something else grabs your attention. Replace the weeds with seeds of rational thoughts.

Shut down the negative static and change the narrative in your mind.

- Take 3 deep breaths, from the depths of your diaphragm. Review your list of negative thoughts.

- Identify the negative static or Resistance that is sapping your confidence. Write a rational rebuttal for each negative thought.

- Build a case for yourself, point by point.

Most problems are solved when we gain the appropriate perspective. This can happen alone, or with a learning partner. A partner can help you identify and work through blind spots and patterns of behavior. You can also get some perspective by spending time doing another activity. Alternative viewpoints are helpful. If weeds continue to be out of control, seek additional help (a mentor, a coach, a therapist).

Develop A Vision

A clear picture of success makes maintenance easier for everyone involved. Visioning is not just for annual planning, but for every goal. If you want an effective meeting, what should that look like?

When used as an ongoing tool, Visioning manifests itself in increasing your individual, team, or organizational ability to not just get stuck on problems that you're dealing with right now, which happens to everyone, but to be able to step back and say, "yes, all these things are going wrong…but, *what would it look like if it were going right?*"

Sounds simple but takes some practice to do. Visioning is not just a statement for the company, though that is important. Visioning is a stance we can take for everything we undertake. Fundamentally, it is taking responsibility for seeing a problem through to the end. Few people start with that clarity of the end result, but we can all usually feel when we haven't reached it.

Form a picture of what success looks like in the future, as a story, with enough richness of detail that we will know when we have arrived. The level of detail is up to us. The key is that everyone involved in helping to make the vision a reality can picture what success looks like and that we know as a group when we got there.

When we think of what success looks like in the future if things were going well, we need to hit four critical elements:

- Inspiring: to everyone involved.

- Strategically sound: if it's not sound, it's fantasy. There needs to be a chance of achieving it.

- Documented: most of the time the vision for success is in the leader's head. Write it down. (Not notes, actual sentences.)

- Communicated: A vision can't scale when only one person is living it and feeling it. Once it's written down, it needs to be shared.

Most often, people get stuck when it comes to documenting, because it feels so big. Then, when it's written down, people feel like it's done. They want to get it off their plate and share it—to just print off 25 copies and say, "OK, it's been communicated." Something to consider at this point is: it needs to be communicated in ways that people will hear it.

Visions are ongoing, living things. We might roll them out to who is there at the time, but we forget to integrate the new people to the company, or reiterate it at every meeting, etc. Every 6 months, there is an opportunity to check and see who has not heard it.

"A hero is an ordinary individual who finds the
strength to persevere and endure in spite
of overwhelming obstacles."

— CHRISTOPHER REEVE,
American actor

"The only thing worse than being blind is
having sight but no vision."

— HELEN KELLER,
American author, political activist, and lecturer

"Anyone can give up; it is the easiest thing
in the world to do. But to hold it together
when everyone would expect you to
fall apart, now that is true strength."

— CHRIS BRADFORD,
American author and black belt martial artist

"To the person who does not know where he wants
to go there is no favorable wind."

— SENECA,
Roman Stoic philosopher, statesman

 Like a seed, we are equipped with everything we need to succeed. Contributions to upward spirals yield seeds; contributions to downward spirals yields weeds. We don't require perfect conditions. In fact, persistence amidst challenge and change is what serves as the catalyst for growth.

 Seeds and weeds need constant cultivation and tending. Meaning, we need to manage our upward and downward spirals. Visioning helps us steady ourselves to an ever-evolving, horizonal goal of success.

 Talk to a friend or trusted colleague about the times when you've both gained strength from your practice. How did you get started? What helped turn it into a consistent habit?

If you keep a journal for your own development, write down your thoughts about the best ways to find the stamina you need to deal more effectively with challenge and change.

Consider your vision for greatness. Be as specific as possible.

____

____

What aspects inspire you?

____

____

Is it strategically sound?

____

____

Write it down. Determine who you will share it with.

____

If you'd like to continue thinking about this idea in the future, check the box

At the end of the book, you can summarize all the practices that worked for you and start to generate your own curriculum.

5

Develop Social Skills

Social skills are more than just being friendly or, as some more resistant to the EQ message put it "being kinder and gentler." Goleman describes social skills as "friendliness with a purpose." We are polite and respectful, and also *intentional*. Healthy relationships can be used for personal and organizational benefit; they can help us advance, develop others, and get things done.

- **Don't compromise…yourself.** It is not easy to take a stand, especially when the stakes are high. Knowing ourselves enough to know what works for us and what doesn't, and integrating those things into our daily practices is what helps us recognize unhealthy compromise when it comes knocking

- **Build bonds.** We get our results by having strong bonds with others. The quality of our relationships can either block or enable our success in projects as well as promotions. The ability to develop and build genuine rapport is critical to personal (and group) effectiveness.

- **Persuade**—the ability to win people to our perspective— comes down to an ability to adjust. We adjust ourselves to provide the right message, to the right people, at the right time to more effectively connect and drive results

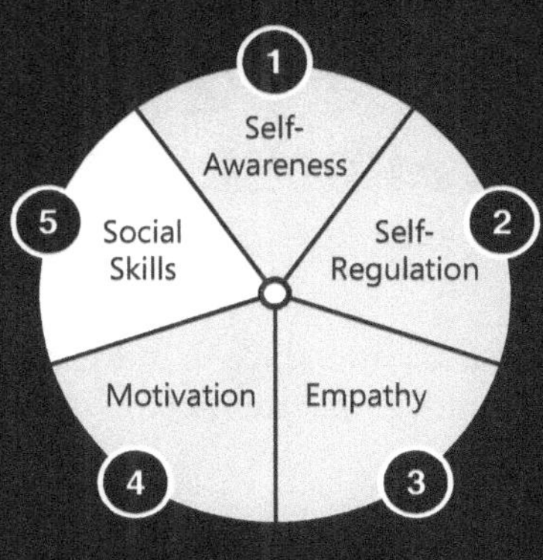

with others. Developing these skills develops our*selves*—specifically, our self-awareness, unique knowledge, and belief in what we're saying.

- **Cooperate**—It's hard enough to cooperate when we work with people in person, let alone across various geographies. Distributed teams are becoming more and more prevalent, making our ability to develop and manage relationships that much more important.

- **Embrace emotional labor.** We practice what we know—over and over—until what we are trying no longer works or has diminishing returns. At that point, we acknowledge that know-how or routine behavior won't help us and we are ready to surrender to another way. When we utilize our inner resources to learn new pathways we innovate. That takes *emotional labor.*

Pressure is all around me to move in a direction I disagree with - what can I do?

There are times when we feel tremendous forces moving us in a particular direction, and we feel like giving in.

In times like these, it's time to understand which people need to be pleased and why—because it's not going to be everyone.

"Can compromise be an art?
Yes—but a minor art."

— Joyce Carol Oates,
American writer

Compromise can be a good thing. It can lead us toward the middle ground and more creative solutions. But when compromise breaks reciprocity, when it impacts our dignity or sense of self, it can be damaging.

Sometimes we find ourselves in situations that provoke use to question our own judgment, or conflict with our personal ethics. Maybe a manager asks us to engage in unethical behavior by faking monthly performance numbers. We might be approached to write a letter of recommendation for someone we do not respect. We are asked to betray the confidence of a colleague. Requests may be made of us that put our reputations or promotions at risk. On these occasions, we may feel tempted to surrender to these external pressures and persuasive personalities.

But something happens when we feel ourselves starting to unravel. Our inner voice starts to speak up, alerting us to mistakes we are about to make.

Integrity is built by small actions over a lifetime, but it can be lost in a moment. That we hold something so precious within each of us means we owe it to ourselves to adopt a certain code or discipline.

When we are pressured to move in a direction that compromises our ethics and values, or the team or organization's ethics or values, if we have made integrity a habit, or practice, then we can choose to not compromise ourselves. Period.

We can stand firm, within reason, and still respect the requestor. We can seek clarity, in writing, about what is actually needed for reporting. Once we truly understand the request, cite values guidelines when denying it. We can then suggest a conversation to understand the real motivations behind the request and offer to brainstorm alternative solutions.

We can deny a letter of recommendation for someone we do not respect by respectfully declining and sharing what went into that decision. It's possible they never knew the true impact they had, and this is a first opportunity to hear feedback from someone they respect. We can offer to remain connected and of service should the person want mentoring, or a sounding board in the future.

If we are asked to betray the confidence of a colleague, or we actually do betray them, we need to brace for the consequences. It's no secret that today's workplace is a competitive environment. Competitive environments drive unethical behavior where people undermine each other to get attention, acknowledgement, or promotions. In the end, any information that you're not prepared to share with everyone in the office probably should not be shared with anyone.

Instead of getting lost by the current pressures around us, our integrity can become the ballast of the group. If we know ourselves, and what we will and won't do, and (most importantly) why… people start turning to us for guidance. Instead of giving in to unreasonable requests, we stand our ground—and we can do that respectfully. Instead of tuning out our conscience when a manager oversteps the line, how can we tune into it and help them succeed?

Easy to say, hard to practice. It is not easy to take a stand, especially when the stakes are high. It can take courage and grit. Knowing ourselves enough to know what works for us and what doesn't, and integrating those things into our daily practices is what helps us recognize unhealthy compromise when it comes knocking.

"You know you're in a bureaucracy
when a hundred people who think 'A'
get together and compromise on 'B'."
— SCOTT ADAMS,
American cartoonist and author

"Compromises have this recommendation,
that if you concede anything, you have
something conceded to you in return."
— HENRY CLAY,
American attorney and statesman

"Every human relationship implies compromises,
but the limit to any compromise
is one's own dignity"
— FAUSTO CERCIGNANI,
Italian scholar, essayist and poet

 It is not easy to take a stand, especially when the stakes are high. Knowing ourselves enough to know what works for us and what doesn't, and integrating those things into our daily practices is what helps us recognize unhealthy compromise when it comes knocking.

 Frame the compromise. Take a moment to define your position (for yourself, first). Observe your thoughts. Recognize negative self-talk, or where you feel you have to go along to get along. Understand what points you will and won't shift in order to understand and meet the other person and their needs. Then find the courage to take a stand.

 Talk to a friend or trusted colleague about which is more important: integrity or popularity. Discuss possible costs of compromising your integrity for short-term gain or a few moments of being considered "in."

If you keep a journal for your own development, write your thoughts about the importance of learning what your position is on a particular issue, and taking a stand.

____

____

____

____

____

____

____

____

____

____

____

____

If you'd like to continue thinking about this idea in the future, check the box

At the end of the book, you can summarize all the practices that worked for you and start to generate your own curriculum.

 I prefer to focus on tasks when meeting with people. I have a hard time connecting on personal details. Sometimes I don't know what to ask or even share about myself, but in the end, I really don't care. I just want to do the work.

 Results are important and maintaining relationships are becoming increasingly critical as organizations become more densely matrixed, geographically dispersed, and virtually managed.

Workplaces are moving toward more cross-disciplined collaboration and consensus-driven decision making, requiring informal networks to work with immediate effectiveness. The ability to develop rapport quickly and genuinely is critical to personal (and group) effectiveness.

 "You can make more friends in
two months by becoming interested
in other people than you can in
two years by trying to get
other people interested
in you."

— DALE CARNEGIE,
American writer and lecturer

People who are good at building bonds with others are great networkers, building and maintaining a strong network of contacts and connections. They are extremely good at generating rapport, but also work on established relationships to keep them healthy. Two characteristics of people who are good at this skill are that they have many friends among their work colleagues. They also tend to keep friends and colleagues across their lives. At its essence, the ability to build and maintain bonds comes down to valuing others: genuinely being interested in them and wanting to know more about them.

In the end, building rapport is about mutual respect. It's a lot like a good tennis game, where the ball is served, and returned. We give, and we want to get, for the purpose of having a good game where each player gives their all. We do not want the other person to miss connecting with the ball, and we do not want them to run off with it. We do not want them to slam a volley and shut the game down. We want a conversation where we are both heard. We want a nice, easy game of back and forth.

Some helpful tactics to building rapport with people are:

- *Know your audience.* Research, but not too much. Social media makes most people an open book. Learning what topics they feel are important, what hobbies and interests they have, or if there are any mutual connections make it easier to build conversation bridges across what might have felt like vast territories of awkwardness.

  At the same time, people don't like to feel stalked. We can lead with things like: "I saw on LinkedIn that …", or "I noticed you tweeted about …", or "I read on your blog that … " as potential openers.

But you don't need to know someone socially to connect. even just asking what is expected at a meeting can help you better orient to the other person's needs.

- *Learn the gift of small talk, but don't force it.* There are some people who can easily sidle up to people like they've been lifelong friends, find humor in the mundane or say something witty, and immediately ingratiate themselves to others.

  Some people find casual conversation stressful, annoying, or inefficient. If the person we are talking so seems uncomfortable answering our questions, remains monotone, or only offers up the shortest of answers, we might do more harm to the relationship than good. Instead, keeping to the task at hand, or mentioning a recent press release from their company, or commenting on their industry experience can help keep the game going.

- *News, weather, sports—but make it regional.* That means we need to strike the balance between highly relatable topics and similarities that draw us close. We live life in our particulars. When we find we share uncommon commonalities, we feel that we fit in more.

"Assumptions are the termites of relationships."
— HENRY WINKLER,
American actor, comedian, director, producer, and author

"When dealing with people, remember you are not dealing with creatures of logic, but creatures of emotion."
— DALE CARNEGIE,
American writer and lecturer

"Do what you can to show you care about other people, and you will make our world a better place."
— ROSALYNN CARTER,
American who served as First Lady of the United States

"When you stop expecting people to be perfect, you can like them for who they are."
— DONALD MILLER,
American author, public speaker

"The meeting of two personalities is like the contact of two chemical substances: if there is any reaction, both are transformed."
— CARL JUNG,
Swiss psychiatrist and psychoanalyst

We get our results by having strong bonds with others. The quality of our relationships can either block or enable our success in projects as well as promotions. The ability to develop and build genuine rapport is critical to personal (and group) effectiveness.

Building bonds is a skill that requires practice. Seek situations outside of work where you can develop relationships—the people who work in your grocery store, the dog park, or your children's school are all great, low-stakes places to start. As you gain confidence, attend networking events. Reframe the experience from needing something to being able to give something to others (advice, contacts, etc.). Brush up on small talk, "what brought you here?" You might walk away with a couple new connections.

Talk to a friend or trusted colleague about how building and maintaining relationships have played a role in your development.

If you keep a journal for your own development, write your thoughts about the importance of building and maintaining relationships, to you. Why is it fundamentally important to you?

____

____

____

____

____

When was the last time you reached out to a former colleague or boss just to stay in touch? say thank you for a lesson learned? request mentoring or a referral?

____

____

____

____

____

If you'd like to continue thinking about this idea in the future, check the box

At the end of the book, you can summarize all the practices that worked for you and start to generate your own curriculum.

I've been told I have to "Lead Without Authority" – how can I make others listen to me when I'm not in charge of them?

Helpful tip: they don't always listen to you when you *are* in charge of them!

As adults, we will do what we want. We can label it as doing what we think is right, but at the end of the day, we do what we want. We are more successful when we are persuasive.

"You don't have to be a 'person of influence'
to be influential. In fact, the most
influential people in my life
are probably not even aware
of what they've taught me."

— Scott Adams,
American cartoonist and author

Persuasion is the art of winning people over to our ideas or proposed course of action. People who are persuasive have influence. They can read the emotional currents in a situation. They can adjust what they are saying to appeal to the right person, with the right message, at the right time.

We can nag, coerce, and chase—but those approaches have quickly diminishing returns. The 'Holy Grail' of persuasion, then, is to get others to buy into the idea, and want to do it your way. And the best way of doing that is in a way that others don't notice. But how?

We can keep our promises, be reliable, generate solutions, and take responsibility when it counts. We can be sincere, genuine, honest, interested, and entertaining. Maybe we are one of those things, maybe we are a few of those things.

The key skills for successful persuasion, then, are pretty wide. People who are persuasive appear confident in themselves and others. They are motivated by the belief their ideas will succeed. They speak with clarity and purpose. They understand their audience because they empathize, listen, and build rapport.

All of these wonderful characteristics fall short if we aren't organized. Knowing ourselves and our subject inside and out helps when we speak with people who have various needs; it helps us connect. We need to have taken time to organize ourselves and think about what outcomes we want to achieve.

Becoming a trusted friend or colleague takes time. Develop these skills, and we start to develop our*selves*. Our innate power and authority to influence others stems from our self-awareness, unique knowledge, and belief in what we're saying. Once we have that, we are likely to be much more effective driving results with others by persuading them, whether at home or at work.

Here is a simple mantra to repeat the next time we confront someone we find challenging: *use my head, have a heart, and lend a hand.*

- Logic is helpful for organizing facts and developing arguments.

- Emotions connect dialogue or decisions to our feelings of well-being or sense of belonging.

- Cooperation involves seeking advice and offering assistance. Collaborating to accomplish a mutually important goal extends a hand to others.

These tactics can be used indirectly or directly.

Applying the Indirect Approach

This approach is a familiar one for most of us because we are saving the main idea for the conclusion. We are leading the other person through a storyline, providing background to conclusion. This is effective with people who are:

- Uninformed and require context or details

- Receptive to our idea but need a little convincing

- Disagree with our idea but willing to hear us out

- Analysis oriented

The indirect approach allows people time to become acquainted with us, our organization and our message before we present our recommendation or request action. An example of when using an indirect approach might be effective is when we are determining a team's vision and values. If dealing with people who disagree with us, or coming from different teams where things were done differently, it gives us time to find common ground.

Applying the Direct Approach

Here, we lead with the "bottom line" and "executive summary." We state the main idea at the beginning of the message. This approach is used for audiences who are:

- Informed and require little context

- Receptive to the message

- Can handle bad news

- Results oriented

The direct approach emphasizes the results of our analysis. It does not focus on the steps we took to get there. Starting with the key points helps people stay focused and give us their attention. It may save time, choosing whether to skim sections of the message, read it carefully or reserve it for reference.

Determining the Approach

A framework adapted from Alan H. Monroe in the early 1960s called "motivated sequence" can help us think through how to apply direct and indirect approaches. Comprised of five steps, it starts with a focus on the benefits of the idea to the result we anticipate. They are Attention, Need, Satisfaction, Visualization, and Action.

1. **Attention**

   The goal is to capture reader interest and present the benefit of the proposed action you are recommending. For example, if you are proposing to move a deadline up significantly, highlight the benefits of an earlier date.

2. **Need**

   Summarize the details or define the boundaries of the problem. Prove that the problem is urgent *and* important. Using the example above, we can cite limitations of a later launch date (cost, competition, etc.), rather than gaining early traction with customers.

3. **Satisfaction**

Share how our solution will eliminate the problems we have identified. Prove the proposed course of action has worked in similar situations. Address objections or alternatives that might come up. Demonstrate how other solutions are less attractive in comparison with our proposal.

4. **Visualize**

Help others see how they will benefit from our proposal. Point out the potential consequences of alternatives. Provide the advantages realized from a decision to follow our advice.

5. **Action**

Provide clarity for the next steps. Most people forget this important step. Confidently state the actions we want. Reiterate the benefits they can expect. Be firm and specific. We should never assume that people know intuitively what actions to take. The result should be an agreement to an earlier launch date.

"Example is not the main thing in influencing others.
It is the only thing."
— Albert Schweitzer,
Alsatian polymath, theologian, writer, and physician

"People exercise an unconscious selection
in being influenced"
— T. S. Eliot,
American essayist, publisher, and literary and social critic

"It takes time to persuade men to do
even what is for their own good."
— Thomas Jefferson,
American statesman, diplomat, lawyer, architect,
and 3rd U.S. President

"If you're trying to persuade people to do something,
or buy something, it seems to me you should use
their language, the language they use every day,
the language in which they think.
We try to write in the vernacular."
— David Ogilvy,
American advertising tycoon, founder of Ogilvy & Mather

 Persuasion—the ability to win people to our perspective—comes down to an ability to adjust. We adjust ourselves to provide the right message, to the right people, at the right time in order to more effectively connect and drive results with others. Developing these skills develops our*selves*—specifically, our self-awareness, unique knowledge, and belief in what we're saying.

 Use your head, have a heart, and lend a hand. Organize information that appeals to attitudes, values, a common purpose, ideals, and beliefs through inspiration or enthusiasm, while collaborating to accomplish a mutually important goal.

 Talk to a friend or trusted colleague about how building and maintaining relationships have played a role in your development.

If you keep a journal for your own development, write
your thoughts about when you last persuaded someone effectively.

____

____

____

____

____

____

What head-heart-hands tactics did you use? Do you
use them all equally?

____

____

____

____

____

If you'd like to continue thinking about this idea in the
future, check the box

At the end of the book, you can summarize all the practices
that worked for you and start to generate your own curriculum.

My organization touts itself as having a collaborative culture, but in reality that collaboration is limited to the overall business goals I'm responsible for. I'm having a hard time driving cooperation across a team that is geographically, functionally, and demographically dispersed. How can I get them to rally around my cause?

While there are some people that will lend a hand no matter what, we tend to cooperate when we understand how the effort will benefit us.

"Because the crew was convinced that I
was "on their team" there were never
any issues with negative criticism…
You as a mentor have to establish
that you are sincerely interested in
the problems of the person
you are mentoring."

— RET. CAPT L. DAVID MARQUET,,
U.S. Naval Captain and author

A choir has many voices. Many hands make light work.
Sticks in a bundle are unbreakable.

We hear these clichés and let out a tired sigh, knowing that we cannot accomplish what we need to alone—even though sometimes it would be easier.

Cooperating in person is challenging. Collaborating virtually is especially challenging. We are already working against barriers of distance, time zones, different cultural perspectives, and language differences. Distance can make it especially hard to share common values through regular interactions, impacting trust and team cohesion. There is the added challenge of establishing norms for communication and knowledge sharing and motivating team members to commit to the team/organization's mission. Virtual teams often have a short-term focus in comparison to their onsite counterparts—though this is starting to change, and fast!

Before we start to think the situation is stacked against us, note that the challenge begins with the task itself. The task informs goals, roles, and frames how you will guide with the team. The task dictates the resources that should be involved. If the assembled resources lack the necessary skills, knowledge, ability, or budget to address the task, we will not be successful. But identifying the right people for the work at hand requires more than just understanding a person's resume; it requires balancing professional chemistry and putting together the right mix of personalities.

Whether we are focused on the short-term or the long-term, our team becomes a self-regulating entity. When chemistry and skills are well matched, relationships are supportive. When they are not, everyone on the team turns into an obstacle in our way. Membership to this team is governed by external and internal social codes. The former is linked to our political capital. If we have become known for not meeting deadlines or producing substandard work, fewer people will want to work with us. There is also the sense of obligation we have to our colleagues. How guilty do we feel at possibly letting others down? Do we have a desire to maintain positive working relationships, or are we all there to just "get it done"?

The answers to these questions, our truest answers, are why our relationships carry true currency—especially over distance. Our effectiveness as a team member or leader is reflective of the micro and macro politics of the organization to which we belong. To grow and meet demands, the organization is constantly shifting, forcing us to adjust. Whether we are successful with our solutions depends on whether our processes are aligned with the tasks. It is limiting to assume that a single, unchanging process is all we will ever need.

That said, cooperation has many ingredients. How can we emphasize the need for and encourage greater cooperation?

- **Advocate for the best fit of team members.** This is especially true for remote team members. Take time to meet and speak with the people who have been nominated for the work and understand their strengths and passions firsthand. Describe the work, and if possible, speak with people who have attempted the work before. If the people you have access to do not seem to be the right fit, discuss replacements with the project's sponsor.

- **Establish norms and process.** We often go right past these tools only to find out later each member held unique assumptions about how the work would be managed. Whenever possible, set team processes that align with the tasks, ensuring that people have the tools necessary to complete their work.

- **Embrace ongoing, intentional communication.** Report status. Celebrate wins. Highlight work of individual team members. This breaks the isolation of the team and celebrates the strengths and accomplishments of the team.

"You can't stay in your corner of the forest waiting
for others to come to you. You have to
go to them sometimes."

— A. A. MILNE,
English author

"In the long history of humankind (and animal kind,
too) those who learned to collaborate and improvise
most effectively have prevailed."

— CHARLES DARWIN,
English naturalist, geologist and biologist

"No matter what your mission is, have some notion in
your head. Forget the model, whether it's government
or nonprofit or profit. Ask yourself the more important question: Is my mission improving the world?
Are you sure about it? Seek to disconfirm that all
the time. And if you can, change your mission."

— JEFF BEZOS,
American businessman, investor, and philanthropist

"We may have all come on different ships,
but we're in the same boat now."

— MARTIN LUTHER KING JR.,
American Christian minister and activist

 It is hard enough to cooperate when we work with people in person, let alone across various geographies. Distributed teams are becoming more and more prevalent, making our ability to develop and manage relationships that much more important.

 Emphasize the need for cooperation by advocating for the best fit of team members, establish norms and process, and be intentional about ongoing communication.

 Talk to a friend or trusted colleague about how building and maintaining relationships have impacted your ability to do your work (whether you were co-located or distributed). What similarities were there in your approach? What differences?

If you keep a journal for your own development, write your thoughts about what you specifically do to maintain relationships once you've started them.

____

____

____

____

____

____

Do you maintain them once you've adjourned on a project? How?

____

____

____

____

____

If you'd like to continue thinking about this idea in the future, check the box

At the end of the book, you can summarize all the practices that worked for you and start to generate your own curriculum.

5

There are challenges that appear "textbook" where I have a ready solution because I've experienced them before. But there are others I don't recognize, or don't see in the books. How can I tackle those?

Our first and most natural response is to try what we know. But there are certain problems where applying current technical know-how or routine behavior doesn't work when driving results with others. The learning in these situations doesn't come from books but requires us to work with what inner resources we have and innovate. That takes *emotional labor*.

"Neurosis is the inability
to tolerate ambiguity."

— Sigmund Freud,
Austrian neurologist and the founder
of psychoanalysis,

Emotional labor is the process of managing feelings and expressions to fulfill the emotional requirements of a job. More specifically, we are expected to regulate our emotions during interactions with others, while performing our day to day tasks: having effective, direct conversations; collaboration when the stakes are high, or speaking to large groups of people with clarity. To perform those skills under pressure is to sit in our own and someone else's discomfort. To be effective, we have to relax our ideas on what the textbook model might or might not work, what we've done before that might or might not work. We must summon the curiosity and the ability to remain in ambiguity for a period of time. Consider the following example.

When Mary saw behavior in a peer or direct and wants to help, the desire might be to share an article, model, or book that helped them when she needed it. This approach rarely works because the other person is not in the same frame of mind as Mary was and does not share the unique circumstances or support that led to the transformational learning she earned. Sure, we can share what has worked for us in the hopes of saving someone else time and energy, but we cannot "hand lessons off" to others and think they will stick. If we want lasting change, we can only create circumstances for someone else's learning. This is what is meant by the advice of "meeting people where they are at." It requires slowing down to have collaborative conversations and the discernment of what to say, when. Leading this kind of change requires the ability for leaders to collaborate with groups and organizations in this same manner in times of intensity. To apply these ideas takes practice, a lot of it.

Using the example of Mary, let's unpack it further.

1. **Look for specific, observable actions.**

   Observing behavior requires us to know the difference be-tween behavior and our judgment of behavior.

2. **State what was observed.**

   Distinguish interpretations about the person's motives, feel-ings, attitudes or personality traits, and implications of why they do what they do.

3. **Remain neutral in observing.**

   A behavior description is non-evaluative. There is no de-termination of an event or action as good or bad, right or wrong. Evaluative statements (such as name calling, accu-sations, and judgments) usually express what the speaker is feeling and convey little about the behavior observed.

Examples

BEHAVIOR DESCRIPTION	INTERPRETATION / EVALUATION
Susan increases the use of her hands when presenting core ideas in a presentation.	Susan is overwhelmed. Susan is desperate, and she's losing her stakeholders the more she waves her hands.
Brian's face gets red, he looks down, and his jaw clenches when I provide feedback on deadlines.	Brian is angry and frustrated. (He might be, but it's still a judgment.)
"Mark, you mischaracterize Sarah's work in meetings when you suggest her contribution to the strategy is marginal."	Mark is a bully. Mark is trying to show Sarah up.

We learn early in our careers that the "sh–t-sandwich" approach to delivery feedback doesn't work. Offering "keep behaviors," or praise, at the same time we're offering "change behaviors," or criticism, we tried to demonstrate that we see performance strengths as well as performance deficits—but really, we just increased confusion and static (and potentially, distrust).

Instead, notice the behaviors that caused you to make a judgment. Lead by stating those behaviors first, *then* own your judgment. *From there*, you can make a request for change. A short conversation script to connect and keep the dialogue moving forward could be:

1. **"I notice that** your deadlines are getting soft."

2. **"The story I'm telling myself is** that you think these commitments don't matter so much."

3. **"I want** you to deliver this project a day in advance, so we aren't scrambling."

There are, of course, more complicated approaches to feedback that are very valid. And this approach will save our bacon more often than we would like to admit.

"Intolerance of ambiguity is the mark of an authoritarian personality."
— THEODOR ADORNO,
German philosopher, sociologist, psychologist and composer

"Life is about not knowing, having to change, taking the moment and making the best of it, without knowing what's going to happen next."
— GILDA RADNER,
American comedian and actress

"What is important is to keep learning, to enjoy challenge, and to tolerate ambiguity. In the end there are no certain answers."
— MATINA HORNER,
American psychologist who was the sixth president of Radcliffe College

"The character of human life, like the character of the human condition, like the character of all life, is "ambiguity": the inseparable mixture of good and evil, the true and false, the creative and destructive forces-both individual and social."
— PAUL TILLICH,
German-American existentialist philosopher and theologian

 We practice what we know—over and over—until what we are trying no longer works or has diminishing returns. At that point, we acknowledge that know-how or routine behavior won't help us and we are ready to surrender to another way. When we utilize our inner resources to learn new pathways we innovate. That takes emotional labor.

 Confronting challenge and change requires our ability to sit with a certain level of discomfort within ourselves and in others. If rules of thumb no longer work, becoming a better observer of behavior can help us find a path. A behavior description is a report of specific, observable actions rather than assumptions, evaluations or interpretations. We block our normal shortcuts to trusted solutions and open ourselves to alternatives. It is focusing on what happened, not why.

 Talk to a friend or trusted colleague about how easy or hard it is to observe and state behaviors in others before you allow yourselves to form judgments. Consider alternatives to those judgments.

If you keep a journal for your own development, write
your thoughts about what feelings come up when
you slow down long enough to observe and name
behaviors in others, versus leaping more quickly to
judgments.

____

____

____

____

____

What did you learn about yourself?

____

____

____

____

____

If you'd like to continue thinking about this idea in the
future, check the box

At the end of the book, you can summarize all the practices
that worked for you and start to generate your own curriculum.

Now that you have explored the 5 Principles of Emotional Intelligence and have put in a little work to reflect and try different tools and strategies from the chapters, you can create your own practice.

The next question is: How? This final question will help answer that question. When you're ready, let's get started.

Design Your Own Practice

As you were learning about Emotional Intelligence and applying it toward driving results through others, you may have experienced benefits from reflection and would like to continue with it. Or, you may have found none of this was for you. You might think all of this was common sense (it is), and you already know most of what's here (you might). If that's the case, that's fine! While I believe that having some kind of reflective practice is helpful to most people, I know that it isn't a fit for everyone. Before moving forward, take some time to think about whether you'd like to continue your practice, and answer honestly.

If you'd like to continue your journey, read on. Not every exercise is a good fit for everyone, and people will wind up in different places while working through the book. Because this isn't a one-size-fits-all solution, the rest of this chapter is dedicated to helping you design your own personalized reflection practice.

STEP 1: Review What Worked.

The first step is to (finally!) put all those boxes you checked at the end of each chapter to use. The table on the following page lists all the exercises from this book. Take some time to go back and find which exercises you checked off and summarize them in the table on the following page.

The exercises are sorted by principle, which will be useful in the next few steps of designing your own practice.

EXAMPLE

BUILD YOUR OWN

X	#	TOPIC TITLES	SELF-AWARENESS	SELF-REGULATION	EMPATHY	MOTIVATION	SOCIAL SKILLS	S-O-C
	1	Opportunities Are Everywhere.	●					
	2	Emotions Teach Us.	●					
	3	Cultivate Perspective.	●					
	4	Using Challenge To Grow.	●					
	5	Be Your Own Guide.	●					
X	6	You Are In Control.		●				S
	7	Maintain Inner Peace.		●				
X	8	Emotions Are Contagious.		●				C
	9	Anger Means Danger.		●				
X	10	Go Beyond Worry.		●				C
	11	Be Compassionate.			●			
X	12	Find Patience.			●			O
X	13	Learn From Everyone, Even Them.			●			O
X	14	Check Your Filters.			●			C
X	15	Ask More Questions.			●			C
	16	Find Stamina.				●		
X	17	Know Your Motivations.				●		S
X	18	Develop A Practice.				●		S
X	19	Focus On The Small.				●		S
	20	Hold Tension.				●		
X	21	Don't Compromise...Yourself.					●	C
	22	Build Bonds.					●	
	23	Persuade.					●	
	24	Cooperate.					●	
X	25	Embrace Emotional Labor.					●	C

KEY
S = Set time
O = Occasionally, when the opportunity arises
C = Constantly, as often as possible

BUILD YOUR OWN

X	#	TOPIC TITLES	SELF-AWARENESS	SELF-REGULATION	EMPATHY	MOTIVATION	SOCIAL SKILLS	S-O-C
	1	Opportunities Are Everywhere.	●					
	2	Emotions Teach Us.	●					
	3	Cultivate Perspective.	●					
	4	Using Challenge To Grow.	●					
	5	Be Your Own Guide.	●					
	6	You Are In Control.		●				
	7	Maintain Inner Peace.		●				
	8	Emotions Are Contagious.		●				
	9	Anger Means Danger.		●				
	10	Go Beyond Worry.		●				
	11	Be Compassionate.			●			
	12	Find Patience.			●			
	13	Learn From Everyone, Even Them.			●			
	14	Check Your Filters.			●			
	15	Ask More Questions.			●			
	16	Find Stamina.				●		
	17	Know Your Motivations.				●		
	18	Develop A Practice.				●		
	19	Focus On The Small.				●		
	20	Hold Tension.				●		
	21	Don't Compromise...Yourself.					●	
	22	Build Bonds.					●	
	23	Persuade.					●	
	24	Cooperate.					●	
	25	Embrace Emotional Labor.					●	

STEP 2: Determine Which Principle To Start From

The main goal of this book is to provide an adequate sampling of practices that will increase your emotional intelligence and help you work more effectively with and through others. Now the question remains: which principle should you start from? While no hard-fast rule exist, increasing self-awareness is generally the best place to begin. Understanding yourself, first, is a necessary step in understanding others.

That said, if you believe you would benefit from understanding Motivation more deeply feel free to start there. Or, if there is a pressing work issue that spikes your emotions but you need to remain calm, check out Self-Regulation. If you choose to start elsewhere, be sure you have a strong reason for doing so, and that you're not simply averse to the suggestion of starting at the beginning, or giving in to your desire to be thought of as someone with high "EQ"—those are clear signs you need more work in the first principle!

STEP 3: Design Your Initial Practice

Now that you've chosen a principle to work with further, you can choose exercises you'd like to practice within that principle. In the table you filled out in Step 1, you'll have noticed that each exercise is labeled with letters.

S: The exercise is meant to be done intentionally at a set time. For example, Develop A Practice, described in Understanding Motivation, requires you to set time aside to practice. This can be done daily, but it doesn't have to be.

O: These exercises are done when the occasion arises for which they are relevant. Keep these exercises in mind, and when the opportunity to practice them comes about, you can do so. Using Be

Compassionate as an example, giving thought to others' adversity requires encountering (or reading or hearing about) a person who is struggling with something. Maybe they are in a culture where harassment is common, where bullying behavior is left unchecked. You would use this cue as a reminder to tell yourself that something similar could easily happen to you.

C: These exercises (or aspects of them) are practiced constantly, or as often as possible. For example, the Going Beyond Worry exercise asks you to reflect on things in and out of your control. You could take this exercise to an extreme and list all the things out of your control, every day. In practice, you'll be applying this practice to certain incidents throughout your day, compared to the other two types of exercises. Meaning it is not that you have a Set Time or do them Occasionally—you are integrating this practice into your life by trying to do it constantly. So instead of worrying about something and reacting, you instead immediately start considering what is in and out of your control. This is how muscle memory is formed, and how impulses can be shifted. This doesn't take a lot of time, but it does take effort.

With that out of the way, it's time to design a practice within your chosen principles. Turn back to the table in Step 1 and look at which principles worked for you, then choose which you'd like to work on for now. Here are some recommendations:

- Keep it simple. Only choose one or two practices to work with at a time. Many people get overwhelmed when confronted with too much choice, so narrowing your practice may be useful.

- For most people, to start, it is recommended to identify one practice that is done at a **set time** and one practice done **occasionally**. Practices at a set time give consistency, and practices done occasionally help you practice in daily life.

- If you struggle with one area in particular within a given principle, choose an exercise relevant to that particular issue to start out with. Begin with a less challenging aspect of your chosen area and increase difficulty with time.

- Stay within your chosen principle until you are ready to move on.

STEP 4: Know When And How To Progress

You won't be using your initial practice forever. So, how will you know when it's time to move on? Here are two ways:

Proceeding to the next practice: There aren't hard and fast rules about figuring out exactly when to move between principles. The most important idea to keep in mind is that individual exercises have only one goal: to help you improve your ability to work through others. Recall the goals of the first two practices:

- Self-awareness: Awareness is about learning to know what we know and feel what we feel. Learn to decrease "social static" by connecting with others in a way that increases our effectiveness.

- Self-regulation: Control and manage our impulses and emotions. Reacting instead of responding can lead to mistakes, less critical thinking, and can often damage relationships.

You can use these as signposts of whether to proceed to the next principle, perhaps by reflecting and journaling about your progress and comparing your progress every few months to your goals within a particular principle. You don't have to be perfect in the first two principles to move ahead, none of us are, but you shouldn't have glaring issues in those areas before proceeding.

Once you meet your goals in one principle, you can then use the tools and suggestions in Step 3 to help guide you in creating a new initial curriculum for the next principle.

Moving On To Other Exercises Within A Principle

Here are some cues to let you know that it may be time to change exercises within a principle:

- If a given exercise does not seem to be working

- If circumstances change and another exercise seems more relevant

- If your overall progress within the discipline seems stagnant, but you haven't met your goals for the principle

- If you'd like to explore new exercises that workd for you in the past

- If the exercise has become second nature to you and you're ready to add a new one within the same principle

- If you've made significant progress in the area addressed by the exercise and want to try a new exercise for a different area of your life.

Try not to rotate exercises too frequently to give them sufficient time to have effect. Switch to exercises that can be done constantly (marked with a C in the tables in Step 1) when you are closer to your goals within a principle, as these tend to be harder but also more beneficial.

Your own personalized curriculum can last months, years, or even a lifetime. In the next and final section, are some additional resources to supplement your study of emotional intelligence and working through others more effectively.

Acknowledgements

*Education is not the learning of facts, but
the training of the mind to think.*

—Albert Einstein

There is nothing quite like learning on the job. Effective management comes with practice. Strong leadership comes from being battle-tested. When the stakes feel high and our patience is running thin, there is little room for a spirit of practice. And that is the critical moment, under pressure to perform, when leaders at all levels need to train their minds to think more effectively.

This book summarizes themes experienced by leaders at all levels, across multiple sectors—from first time managers to seasoned veterans. I hope it provides a perspective that while many people experience these challenges, struggling with them isn't a requirement. And, once you learn what approaches are most effective for you, this resource offers guidance on how to create your own reflective practice so you can train your mind to think more effectively.

No work is ever done alone. There were many people who supported me through this little pocket-guide series, helping me gnash through ideas, outlines, and experiences to tell a more coherent story. Enormous thanks to Steve, whose belief in me never wavers.

There were people who offered everything from tremendous emotional support for my endeavors in providing observations, insightful questions, and challenging feedback on early versions

Acknowledgements

of the work: Marsha Kabacov, Diane Wagner, Jan Monti, and Lara Hanson.

To John Hinds, Amy Morgan, Shelley Roberts your friendship and comments have directly influenced this overall work.

Thanks to Rob Nance for everything graphical and lovely; I've appreciated your guidance in the process.

To all the clients I've worked with who generously shared a slice of their life experiences with me: thank you for bringing this series to life. You are smart, talented, and generous. I never reference specific clients for privacy reasons—but you know who you are! It's my honor to venture into the sometimes-rough neighborhoods of your minds alongside you and to help re-frame your thoughts in a way that moves you forward. The transformations you experience continue to inspire me in helping people to first learn how to become their own best advocates. Only then, can they reach their goals and tap their innate potential.

Thank you for reading—I will be your biggest cheerleader and advocate wherever you go from here. My hope is that you develop and learn strategies that help you exceed your own expectations of yourself.

Take good care,

Christine Haskell, PhD

Resources

The emphasis throughout this book has been on practice. In making that choice, practicing without theory is blind, and it risks turning basic psychological and philosophical principles into a bag of tricks. Tricks—or more charitably, techniques—can work for specific purposes, and there is nothing wrong if you wish to limit yourself to those purposes.

But how do you arrive at your learning purpose? Being a real lifelong learner, as many of us want to claim to be, provides an answer to this question. The techniques in this book are derived from basic psychological or philosophical theory. The dichotomy of control is rooted in Stoic philosophy. Empathy, motivation and exploration of emotions come from the roots of psychology.

So while the suggestions presented in this book are meant to help you continue your practice, it only covers the application part of the learning. Here are some resources for those interested in digging a little deeper.

- Chödrön, P. (2001). *Start where you are: A guide to compassionate living.* Boston: Shambhala.

- Chödrön, P. (1997). *When things fall apart: Heart advice for difficult times.* Boston, MA: Shambhala.

- Collins, J. C. 1., & Hansen, M. T. (2011). *Great by choice: uncertainty, chaos, and luck : why some thrive despite them all.* New York, NY: HarperCollins Publishers.

- Csikszentmihalyi, M. (1990). *Flow: The psychology of optimal experience.* New York: Harper & Row.

- Boyce, T. (2019). *The Orchid and the Dandelion: Why Sensitive Children Face Challenges and How All Can Thrive.* New York, NY: Penguin Random House.

- Frankl, V. E. (1984). *Man's search for meaning: An introduction to logotherapy.* New York, NY: Simon & Schuster.

- Dweck, C. S. (2006). *Mindset: The new psychology of success.* New York: Random House.

- Goldsmith, M. (2015). *Triggers: Creating Behavior That Lasts—Becoming the Person You Want to Be.* New York, NY: Crown Publishing Group.

- Goleman, D. (1995). *Emotional Intelligence: Why It Can Matter More Than IQ.* New York, NY: Bantam Books.

- Grandin, T. & Johnson, C. *Animals in Translation: Using the Mysteries of Autism to Decode Animal Behavior.* New York, NY: Harcourt, Inc.

- Harris, N. B. (2018). *The Deepest Well: Healing the Long-Term Effects of Childhood Adversity.* New York, NY: Houghton Mifflin Harcourt.

- Harris, D. & Adler, C. (2017). *Meditation for fidgety skeptics : a 10% happier how-to book.* New York, NY: Spiegel & Grau.

- Heen, S. & Stone, D. (2015). *Thanks for the feedback: the science and art of receiving feedback well (even when it is off base, unfair, poorly delivered, and, frankly, you're not in the mood).* UK: Portfolio Penguin.

- Heifetz, R. A. (1994). *Leadership without easy answers.* Boston, MA: Harvard Business School Press.

Resources

- Kaster, R. A. & Nussbaum, M.C. (2012). *Seneca: Anger, Mercy, Revenge.* University of Chicago Press.

- Kegan, R., & Lahey, L. L. (2009). *Immunity to change: How to overcome it and unlock potential in yourself and your organization.* Boston, Mass: Harvard Business Press.

- Marcus, A., & Hays, G. (2002). *Meditations.* New York: Modern Library.

- Maslow, A. H. (1954). *Motivation and personality.* New York: Harper and Row. Maslow, A. H. (1962).

- Rogers, C. R. 1. (1961). *On becoming a person: a therapist's view of psychotherapy.* Boston: Houghton Mifflin.

- van der Kolkm, B. (2014). *The Body Keeps the Score: Brain, Mind, and Body in the Healing of Trauma.* New York, NY: Penguin Books.

About the Author

Leaders must summon the courage to see what others cannot and say what needs to be said; to sit amidst their own discomfort as well as others and live with the strength that comes from both failure and success—all of which require the ability to drive results with others in the background and the foreground.

Christine Haskell, PhD is a seasoned technology veteran, leadership coach, and adjunct professor. For over twenty years, she has been at the nexus of technology and innovation, at every stage in a company's growth cycle. She has developed first-generation products (Yahoo!, RealNetworks) and lead division-wide, global programs (Microsoft, Starbucks) in both startup and established software, internet, and software-as-service companies.

As a trained social scientist, she observes patterns and makes connections between behaviors and goals. She is known for blending directness with humor and compassion. Elevating organizational capabilities and supporting systems differentiates her work. She achieves consistent results by emphasizing real business creativity in the use of systems, defining a clear and compelling ROI, and by helping both leaders and stakeholders integrate and evolve business processes.

OTHER BOOKS IN THIS SERIES

For the past several years Christine has worked with busy leaders giving them practical tools for the obstacles, conflicts, tensions that come up every day. What if managers and leaders could self-reflect, redirect their behaviors to become more effective?

Self-awareness is a foundation skill in need of intentional, active cultivation. Each book provides topic-specific tools, exercises and information to continue your growth and development.

Driving Your Self Discovery

It has been said, 'that which is shareable is bearable.' Conversations in coaching create the possibility of learning how to be graceful with our vulnerability while moving creatively through life. Learn the differences between therapy and coaching. Observe how what we experience in our lives turn into patterns that influence our present and future. Explore and reflect on the qualities of an effective advocate. Reflect on real-world case studies to understand common problems clients face, the concepts they learned, and how things changed as a result. Use reflection questions throughout the book to help you identify qualities important to you in a coach, to help you pinpoint potential issues for discussion—and start your introspection process prior to working with a coach who is grounded in management experience, the basic principles of psychology, and understands how organizational systems work.

Driving Change During Difficult Times

Most leaders advance initially because they are good at what they do, not necessarily because they understand people. Focusing on the processes and activities needed to complete a project will only ever get us so far. Understanding how people are affected by those processes and projects helps reduce the uncertainty that can lead to anxiety, confusion, and resistance from the people on the ground who may not fully understand the need for the changes or how to adopt and adapt to new processes. Without buy-in from the rest of the organization, a project's outcomes can fall flat. This guide pulls together over 30 approaches and reflections organized against central change management principles: awareness, desire, knowledge, ability, and reinforcement. Each concept is illustrated by common issues faced by both first-time managers and executives, as they navigate the small and large changes of their day-to-day. People applying these tools continually, will see change in how they respond versus react when the pressure is on, how they take the extra effort to cultivate empathy in order to collaborate, and how they start to advocate for themselves more constructively.

The books in this series emphasize skills learned on the job, where we develop a "feel" for our work. To learn well requires the rigor of self-reflection, a commitment to critical thinking, and the development of an intentional learning practice. Each book provides reflections and a way for the reader to develop their own learning curriculum.

Theory, models, and catchphrases to "do more of this or that" just don't cut it. Reflection without purpose doesn't drive results. By practicing the tools in these books, we train our minds to perform better under pressure. We can increase the quality of our thinking to drive better decision making and bottom-line results when the stakes are high.

GIVE THIS TO SOMEONE THAT COULD BENEFIT FROM COACHING

The guides in this series are innovative, road-tested tools that can change behavior by helping people to understand the link between how people frame challenge and change in the workplace as part of a larger pattern. By slowing down to check what data they are selecting to form assumptions and codify beliefs—they can make better decisions, take more informed actions, and increase their leadership effectiveness.

"Deeply scrutinizing some of the smallest interactions with Christine led to profound insights for me about what I bring to an interaction." –**Director, Instagram**

"I tried some of Christine's suggestions with my wife first, to practice, and she immediately saw a change in how I engaged with her. I tried it with someone I was experiencing conflict with at work and it really helped." –**Senior Director, Facebook**

"Working with Christine using some of these tools has been one of the single, most impactful development activities I've engaged in." –**Senior Creative Director, Microsoft**

"Christine distills the essentials of managing and leading to short, easy to find tools and strategies that stretch your comfort zone. Choosing just a few to focus on helped me twofold. I provided more effective support to my employees and co-workers. And, I learned how to better coach myself." –**Superintendent, U.S. Naval Shipyard**

You can learn more at **www.christinehaskell.com/books** or contact Christine directly at **hello@christinehaskell.com**